RichThoughts
for Breakfast
Volume 9

Harold Herring

President of The Debt Free Army
& RichThoughts TV

www.HaroldHerring.com

Debt Free Army
PO Box 900000, Fort Worth, TX 76161

RichThoughts for Breakfast Volume 9
by Harold Herring

ISBN: 978-0-9831779-5-1
Copyright © 2019 by the Debt Free Army
PO Box 900000, Fort Worth, TX 76161
817-222-0011
harold@haroldherring.com

Unless otherwise noted, Scripture references are taken from the King James Version of the Bible.

Please obtain consent of the Author prior to any reproduction, whether in whole or in part, in any form.

Printed in the United States of America.
All rights reserved.

RichThoughts for Breakfast
Volume 9
Table of Contents

Day	Title	Page
1	Is This Your Sign?	7
2	7 Ways to Make the Most of What You've Got	15
3	11 Reasons to Keep Your Ego in Check	24
4	The Missing Ingredient	32
5	That's a Slap in the Lord's Face	42
6	7 Reasons to Know Where You're At	51
7	7 Things We Can Expect from God	59
8	7 Ways to Overcome Negative Stuff	68
9	How to Be Well-Pleasing to God	76
10	You've Got What They've Got	84
11	7 Ways to Hush Your Circumstances	92
12	10 Things You Need to Know About Deception	100
13	God Is Looking for Real Men	110
14	Fight to Win	118
15	God's Economic Forecast	126
16	25 Ways to Know if You're Ready for a Miracle	133
17	A Hamburger Short of a Happy Meal	142
18	What Your Inheritance Should Include	151
19	God Wants Us to Win Every Time	159
20	Ways to Keep a Good Thing Going	167
21	Worthy to Escape	175
22	Are You on the Guest List?	182
23	Four Rivers Flowing Out of Eden	189
24	What Did You Say That Word Was?	197
25	Ignorant ... Stupid ... or Just Naïve	206
26	Can I Get a Witness in the House?	213
27	The Truth About Mammon	220
28	No Second Guessing About Good Living	227

Is This Your Sign?

Day 1

I was standing in a hardware store ... which in and of itself ... is an unusual place for me to be. Just ask my fine wife, Bev.

But maybe I should explain. I told Bev before we were married that *I'd take her places she'd never been, do things she never dreamed of* ... but if something broke down, somebody else was going to fix it. For more than four decades of marriage ... I've kept my word.

In fact, someone called our home on one occasion and asked Bev if I was handy. She said, *"No, but he's close to the phone, if you'd like to speak with him."*

So it is noteworthy if you ever hear that I'm standing in a hardware store of any description.

On this particular day, I was on a mission ... it wasn't from God but it was for my fine wife. While wandering through the aisles I came across *a spinning rack with the various signs, and the Lord sparked my imagination.*

As I've reflected on some of those signs ... I feel led

7

to relate them to the human experience or our spiritual life.

BEWARE OF DOG

Sadly, a lot of churches have Rottweilers and Pit Bulls ... no disrespect intended to the dogs ... people who are easily offended and loud ... ready to *throw down and duke it out.*

Philippians 3:2 in the Message Bible says:

> "Steer clear of the barking dogs, those religious busybodies, all bark and no bite. All they're interested in is appearances—knife-happy circumcisers, I call them. The real believers are the ones the Spirit of God leads to work away at this ministry, filling the air with Christ's praise as we do it ..."

It is important to note that *no self-respecting sign display would be complete without a variety of "BEWARE OF DOG" signs.*

FOR SALE

Are you for sale ... do your values, principles and beliefs have a price?

The "For Sale" sign indicates that something is available for the highest bid or a specific price.

Sadly, too many people ... young and old ... are for

sale. *I'm not talking about human trafficking or sexual liaisons which are bad enough.*

I'm speaking of people who are sitting with co-workers at lunch and someone tells a dirty joke and they laugh along with everyone else ... *they may think they are just appeasing the crowd, but they just sold their witness.*

Employees who call themselves Christian but *take home everything from ink pens and paperclips to file folders or anything else that seems harmless and insignificant* ... have just sold their principles for a pittance.

For those who have sex outside of the marriage bed with their boy/girlfriend regardless of how long they've been dating or how seemingly sweet the words of love ... *they just sold their virtue.*

Taking income without reporting it on your taxes ... *running a red light or breaking any other traffic law because there's nobody around* ... if you take credit for something you didn't do at work or school ... then your principles are FOR SALE.

In reality, if we compromise with sin in any capacity ... *seemingly small or big ... we've just sold our soul and we should have a FOR SALE sign placed around our neck* ... we have to think so we don't abandon our heartfelt principles.

PRIVATE PROPERTY

This is another sign that was spinning around on the rack.

<u>First</u>, it's important ... *<u>absolutely essential that you, I and every other believer fully understand that even though our name is on the deed to our house and cars, they don't belong to us</u>*. And I'm not just talking about the bank holding the note.

<u>Second</u>, in God's economy, we own nothing, but we get to manage everything.

So here's another observation and a question. The tangible private property that you're in charge of ... how effectively are you acting and reacting as a family steward?

The money to which you've been entrusted ... how are you handling God's private property?

Are you spending His money ... His private property ... on foolish pursuits or world-enticed pleasures?

Do you ask Him before spending His money?

Did He really want you to buy that 64-inch Flat Screen High Def TV on 54 monthly payments?

Did He answer "yes" when you asked Him about purchasing the $90,000 motor home for your yearly vacation?

If those things aren't at your home, think about what is. _We all have something that tempts us to lose our focus_.

Third, _God is not against us having things ... He just doesn't want the things having us_.

If where you _live_ ... what you _drive_ ... what you _wear_ ... or what _others think_ about it ... _is more important to you than what He thinks_ ... then you've forgotten whose property you're managing.

On a non-financial note ... _if you allow someone other than your spouse to have access to your physical body_ ... that's a violation of personal property ... because your body is not your own ... it belongs to God.

1 Corinthians 6:19 in the Amplified Bible says:

> "Do you not know that your body is the temple (the very sanctuary) of the Holy Spirit Who lives within you, Whom you have received [as a Gift] from God? You are not your own."

The next two signs are ones that I can honor in the natural ... but not in a spiritual dimension.

NO FISHING

OK, I could promise not to fish for bass, perch or any other aquatic species in your lake, pond, stream or whatever.

But when it comes to the kind of fishing talked about in Matthew 4:19, I feel very differently:

> *"And he saith unto them, Follow me, and I will make you fishers of men."*

The scripture is very clear ... *if you are a follower of Jesus then you are to be a fisher of men.* PERIOD. PARAGRAPH.

My elderly father is one of the greatest fishermen I know. He's led over 70 people a year to the Lord over 14 or 15 years.

I remember calling my Dad on a recent birthday ... in fact, I called him four times that day ... but I will always remember the last conversation. *I asked him what <u>the best thing was about his birthday</u> ... he said that he went fishing.* Even though my parents live on a lake ... I knew that was not the kind of fishing he was talking about.

You guessed it ... my Dad led someone to the Lord on his birthday.

Bottom line ... <u>you may not feel that you're called to be a soul winner but just know that God called you to be one whether you feel like or it not</u>.

One of the best ways to be a soul winner is to live the God-kind of life and let His love and light shine through you.

There is one more sign I saw that I cannot agree to obey spiritually.

NO HUNTING

I'm continually on the hunt to shoot down negative thinking; debt seducers; credit card crack dealers; and the devil of debt and lack.

<u>**I'm pumped, primed, locked and loaded for every trick, trap, lie, deception and wile the enemy is using against the children of God.**</u>

In fact, <u>my passion, my commitment is to place "POSTED" and "NO TRESPASSING" signs on the door of every believer *who has been or is being tempted by the slew foot of unnecessary spending*</u>.

I make no bones about it ... **I'm a Holy Ghost Hunter searching for the good life.**

Proverbs 21:21 in the Message Bible says:

> *"Whoever goes hunting for what is right and kind finds life itself—glorious life!"*

That's such a great scripture ... the sign that you've headed to a good and glorious life is when you pick up the Word of God ... holding on to His promises and provisions.

The last sign is one we're all familiar with ... but are we living it?

WELCOME

The Lord wants us to be a welcome sign for those who've lost their way.

There will come a day when *we will be judged for how we welcomed those we've come in contact with* and only we can answer how well we've done our job or perhaps where we need to improve.

It is amazing how God can use a sign to point us in the right direction. It's good to be able to read the signs of the times.

Harold Herring

Day 2

7 Ways to Make the Most of What You've Got

Here are 7 Ways to Make the Most of What You've Got.

#1 — Use the Ability You've Got.

President Theodore Roosevelt said:

> "Do what you can, with what you have, where you are."

You should always start where you are … **with what you've got** … at the moment.

First, you must know that **you have the God-given ability to perform at a level you never previously thought possible.**

Romans 12:6 in The Living Bible says:

> "God has given each of us the ability to do certain things well …"

This empowerment is a gift from the Holy Spirit.

2 Timothy 1:14 in The Living Bible says:

> "Guard well the splendid, God-given ability you received as a gift from the Holy Spirit who lives within you."

Second, according to Matthew 25:15, each of the three servants were given talents *"according to their several ability."*

What you have at the moment is what you can handle ... but I believe, and more importantly, God knows *you can handle more with a little more understanding.*

Remember, start with what you have ... where you are ... and make the best of it.

Third, you may not have the educational and/or vocational training required for the next position or job you desire. However, **don't complain about what you don't have but use what you do have.** *Create a plan to get from where you are to where you want to be.*

#2 — What Are You Doing When the Boss Isn't Looking?

Two of the three servants in the parable of the talents did what was necessary to earn interest and double the talents they were given.

The third servant buried his talent ... *and went fishing every day until his boss returned.* He was not working

... or *doing anything to prove himself an effective steward of the talents or abilities he was given.*

How many employees go to work every day and do the absolute minimum ... just enough to keep them from getting fired?

Yet, they wonder why they never receive promotions ... and attribute their lack of advancement to the prejudice of their supervisor or boss.

It's always somebody else's fault ... not their own. Yet, the reality is ... their failure to be promoted is simply because of *what they didn't do when the boss wasn't looking.*

Here's a powerful scriptural truth for the workplace, marketplace and every place you live.

Ecclesiastes 12:14 in God's News Translation says:

"God is going to judge everything we do, whether good or bad, even things done in secret."

If you've agreed to work for a company and purposely don't give them your best efforts ... you are planning evil.

#3 — Maximizing Opportunities ... Is a Decision.

The first two servants in Matthew 25 DECIDED to maximize the opportunities they were given. Whereas, the third servant didn't.

There are defining moments in our careers and lives ... **where we are given, take or seize the opportunity to change our destiny.**

I believe the first two servants were very happy to be given the opportunity to prove themselves to their Master. They seized the moment and the opportunity they had been given.

Galatians 6:10 in the New International Version says:

> "Therefore, as we have opportunity, let us do good to all people, especially to those who belong to the family of believers."

Ephesians 5:15-16 in the New International Version says:

> "Be very careful, then, how you live — not as unwise but as wise, making the most of every opportunity, because the days are evil."

Colossians 4:5-6 in the New International Version says:

> "Be wise in the way you act toward outsiders; make the most of every opportunity."

As unbelievable as it may sound, there are some people who sleep away their God-given opportunities in a bed or a cubicle.

Proverbs 10:5 in The Living Bible says:

> "A wise youth makes hay while the sun shines, but what a shame to see a lad who sleeps away his hour of opportunity."

Francis Bacon, the English philosopher, scientist, statesman and author said:

> **"A wise man will make more opportunities than he finds."**

#4 — Pursue Every Opportunity with Excellence.

The first two servants were determined to make their Master proud *and to exhibit a spirit of excellence in what they did.*

God is looking for excellence in effort. *Even the most seemingly meaningless task should be vigorously pursued.*

Matthew 5:16 in the Amplified Bible says:

> *"Let your light so shine before men that they may see your moral excellence and your praiseworthy, noble, and good deeds and recognize and honor and praise and glorify your Father Who is in heaven."*

Excellence is one of the character traits that as believers we're to vigorously pursue.

#5 — Never Compare Your Situation or Opportunity With That of Others.

Nowhere in Matthew 25 do we read where the servant who got two talents complained about *why he didn't get five talents like the first servant.*

The second servant was happy with what he got ... and proved himself worthy of the trust he was given ... by doubling it for the Master.

Do you compare yourself with others ... fellow employees and/or friends ... and complain when they receive something you didn't ... opportunity or otherwise?

Galatians 6:4-5 in God's WORD Translation says:

> *"Each of you must examine your own actions. Then you can be proud of your own accomplishments without comparing yourself to others. Assume your own responsibility."*

This means that you are accountable for your actions ... what you do or don't do. How you act and react. What you say and don't say. You can't blame anybody else for your actions.

When you know that you've done the best job possible ... then is no need to compare yourself to anybody else.

#6 — Don't Bury Your Opportunities.

The third servant must have been a negative dude.

He was lazy, made excuses, questioned authority, was afraid to do what he was asked and failed to increase what he was given ... plus he buried the talent that he was given.

Matthew 25:18 in the Amplified Bible says:

> *"But he who had received the one talent went and dug a hole in the ground and hid his master's money."*

You're probably saying to yourself right about now that you would never have buried the Master's talent.

Before we let go of that thought ... perhaps we should really think it through.

If God has given you the ability to write meaningful words ... to lead and you're not leading ... to teach His Word and you're not teaching ... to give and you're not giving ... then you've buried your talent.

I could go on ... but the real point is simply this ... if you've been burying your talents ... STOP IT ... RIGHT NOW!

<u>Your gifts, abilities and talent (money) are from God ... what you do with it (them) is your gift to Him</u>.

#7 — How to Get the Promotion With Benefits.

All three servants were given a test ... two of them

passed and were blessed with increased benefits.

The third servant failed the test and literally went to hell for it. Not trying to offend your sensitivities ... but that's exactly where he ended up in the scripture.

Someone once defined hell as the day the person you became meets the person you could have become.

Sadly, like the third servant there are way too many believers who are placing limitations in their lives ... limitations which God will never place on you.

Mark 9:23 in the God's Word Translation says:

> "Jesus said to him, 'As far as possibilities go, everything is possible for the person who believes.'"

This scripture ignites my faith and stirs my spirit to new levels of expectation:

> *"... everything is possible for the person [that's me!; that's you!] who believes."*

There is no limitation to our manifestation.

The Message Bible translation of Mark 9:23 says:

> "Jesus said, 'If? There are no "ifs" among believers. Anything can happen.'"

Harold Herring

All things are possible ... anything ... no matter how illogical to the natural mind ... can happen in our lives ... as we exercise our faith and believe.

11 Reasons to Keep Your Ego in Check

How's your nose today?

By that I mean, *which direction does it point?*

When you're climbing the social ladder, does your nose point up ... so you can look down it at the people ... you're leaving behind?

Or does your nose point down ... as you *encourage those behind you to follow you to the top?*

Have you ever had a boss that thought he or she was better than his or her employees?

Rather than congratulate their employees for making him or her a success, the boss took all the glory home at the end of the day ... *and the biggest paycheck, the fancy car, and the fine home.*

Ouch! That's not a place I ever want to work.

Arrogance is outside the will of God.

God says we are to *stop putting ourselves above those around us.*

The Word of God says we are to be humble. <u>We are to place others above ourselves</u>.

In fact, there is no place in the life of the Christian ... for looking down our noses at other people. God will never bless our homes ... our jobs ... our investments ... so long as we keep our nose stuck in the air.

The Word says ... we are rewarded ... for *curbing our out-sized sense of worth.*

Here are **11 Reasons to Keep Your Ego in Check** ... *taken from the Word of God.*

Reason No. 1:

Mahatma Gandhi, the leader of the Indian independence movement, once said:

"When the ego dies, the soul awakes."

The truth is ... you grow closer to God *when you fade into the background.* Less of us ... allows God to bless us ... with *all the good things he desires to give us.*

Matthew 5:5 in the English Standard Version says:

"Blessed are the meek, for they shall inherit the earth."

Reason No. 2:

Pride gets in the way ... of discovering *what God wants for you.*

If you want to make God happy ... try <u>leaving your pride in your sock drawer each morning</u>. Your humble footwear makes you a better person.

Psalm 149:4 in the English Standard Version says:

> "For the Lord takes pleasure in his people; he adorns the humble with salvation."

Reason No. 3:

God has his eyes on his people ... and *that means you*.

If you want to please God ... and you should ... <u>read your Bible ... do what it says</u>.

Isaiah 11:4 in the English Standard Version says:

> "But with righteousness he shall judge the poor, and decide with equity for the meek of the earth ..."

Reason No. 4:

Tossing out your ego ... allows *praise to take* a foothold in your life.

You will find your time with God ... will be the *best time of your day.*

Psalm 22:26 in the English Standard Version says:

> "The afflicted shall eat and be satisfied; those who seek him shall praise the Lord! May your hearts live forever!"

Psalm 22:26 in the Amplified Bible (AMP) says:

> "The afflicted will eat and be satisfied; Those who [diligently] seek Him and require Him [as their greatest need] will praise the Lord. May your hearts live forever!"

Reason No. 5:

Edith Wharton, American novelist and winner of the Pulitzer Prize once said:

> **"There are two ways of spreading light: to be the candle or the mirror that reflects it."**

God's riches are found in your relationship with Him ... even if you're struggling with getting by to the end of the month ... *God hasn't forgotten how much He loves you.*

He wants you ... to *reflect His love and joy* ... <u>to everyone you meet</u>.

Isaiah 29:19 in the English Standard Version says:

> "The meek shall obtain fresh joy in the Lord, and the poor among mankind shall exult in the Holy One of Israel."

I especially like Isaiah 29:19 in the Good News Translation (GNT):

> "Poor and humble people will once again find the happiness which the Lord, the holy God of Israel, gives."

Insert your name in this verse.

> "[[Your Name Here]] will once again find the happiness which the Lord, the holy God of Israel, gives."

Reason No. 6:

Do you want to be beautiful ... <u>really beautiful</u> ... in God's eyes?

God finds your beauty in your spirit ... and you will <u>become beautiful to the people around you too</u>.

1 Peter 3:4 in the English Standard Version says:

> "But let your adorning be the hidden person of the heart with the imperishable beauty of a gentle and quiet spirit, which in God's sight is very precious."

Reason No. 7:

Muhammad Ali, boxing great, once said:

> "I hated every minute of training, but I said, 'Don't quit. Suffer now and live the rest of your life as a champion.'"

You can be on top ... or you can slide to the bottom.

God says to pick a side ... His side ... strive for righteous living ... and He will *adorn you with honor and glory*.

Psalm 147:6 in the English Standard Version says:

> *"The Lord lifts up the humble; he casts the wicked to the ground."*

Reason No. 8:

Seek righteousness ... and humility ... and <u>God's protecting hand will cover you</u>.

Your every footstep will be in the shadow of the Almighty.

Zephaniah 2:3 in the English Standard Version says:

> *"Seek the Lord, all you humble of the land, who do his just commands; seek righteousness; seek humility; perhaps you may be hidden on the day of the anger of the Lord."*

Reason No. 9:

An arrogant man or woman can't see any way ... but their own.

You are useless to God ... *when He can't mold you to his plan.*

Psalm 25:9 in the English Standard Version says:

> "He leads the humble in what is right, and teaches the humble his way."

Reason No. 10:

A pebble in your shoe ... makes you a touchy person.

Put on your Dr. Scholls and you'll wear a smile on your face. (smiling)

Proverbs 15:1 in the English Standard Version says:

> "A soft answer turns away wrath, but a harsh word stirs up anger."

Reason No. 11:

Patrick Henry, American patriot, once said:

> "This is all the inheritance I give to my dear family. The religion of Christ will give them one which will make them rich indeed."

God says your attitude ... *and your gratitude* ... will earn you peace.

Psalm 37:11 in the English Standard Version says:

"*But the meek shall inherit the land and delight themselves in abundant peace.*"

So, back to our original question ... how's your nose?

Where's it aimed? In the air ... where you can trip and fall over any obstacle the devil wants to put in your way ... *or are you willing to eat humble pie* ... <u>and be the Christian God wants you to be</u>?

Your ego can never come first. Toss it out the window ... hide it in a drawer ... do whatever it takes.

You must always let Jesus take first place.

The Missing Ingredient

I remember like it was yesterday ... the day ... the Lord gave me three words ...

"The Missing Ingredient."

I had just sat down to begin my Daily Bible Reading when the Lord directed me to 1 Thessalonians 5:11 in the New International Version which says:

> "Therefore encourage one another and build each other up, just as in fact you are doing."

As I re-read the verse, He stirred the three words in my spirit once again

THE MISSING INGREDIENT.

I asked the Lord what He meant and here's what He said to me:

> "Encouraging others in the Word is the missing ingredient to success and prosperity."

He went on to say that many of *His children who*

want to prosper have the wrong focus. **Instead of keeping their eyes on Him and those He wants to bless ...** *they focus on themselves and their own needs.*

Once again my spirit was stirred as I read the Message Bible translation of 1 Thessalonians 5:11 which says:

> *"Build up hope so you'll all be together in this, no one left out, no one left behind. I know you're already doing this; just keep on doing it."*

He immediately and specifically drew my attention to "**... no one left out, no one left behind ...**"

I'm *not saying that we don't encourage one another as friends* and fellow believers but it's all *too often either convenient and/or self-serving encouragement.*

Have you ever told someone they looked nice ... <u>just so they would think good thoughts toward you</u>?

I realize that some ... perhaps most of you reading this today ... are probably saying to yourself ... **"No, I'd never do that."**

Have you ever had a spouse or a friend who asked you how they looked? Did you always tell the truth ... or were you *just being nice to make them feel good or avoid conflict or both?*

Have you ever read something that a friend wrote ... **whether it was a poem or an article ... and you told them it was good, when in fact, it wasn't?**

*Have you ever complimented someone at work **just so they would like and appreciate you more**?*

Have you ever, as the saying goes, **flattered a teacher or your boss**?

There is a **difference between flattery and encouragement**.

First, it's very clear how God feels about flattery.

Job 32:22 in the New Living Translation says:

> "For if I tried flattery, my Creator would soon destroy me."

Second, Jesus didn't like flattery ... especially from religious folks.

Mark 11:43 in The Message version of the Bible says:

> "You're hopeless, you Pharisees! Frauds! You love sitting at the head table at church dinners, love preening yourselves in the radiance of public flattery. Frauds! You're just like unmarked graves: People walk over that nice, grassy surface, never suspecting the rot and corruption that is six feet under."

The Word says that people who use **flattery often have ulterior motives**.

1 Thessalonians 2:5 in the New Living Translation says:

> *"Never once did we try to win you with flattery, as you well know. And God is our witness that we were not pretending to be your friends just to get your money!"*

If you carefully read Proverbs 7 and substitute the word "debt" for "prostitute" … you will see that this analogy shows rather clearly **how the world will do anything to lure unsuspecting believers into their tangled web of debt and bondage**.

Read in Proverbs 7:5 in the New Living Translation:

> *"So she seduced him with her pretty speech and enticed him with her flattery."*

The world of commercials appeals to our sensual nature *because they try to seduce believers and others with enticing offers.*

Advertisers <u>**use inviting words to make people think their product will give them a lifestyle like the rich and famous**</u>.

But lest I stray let me get back to **the missing ingredient**.

According to dictionary.com the word flattery is defined as:

> "a flattering compliment or speech; excessive, insincere praise."

The missing ingredient is not *flattery* but *encouragement*.

According to Webster's Unabridged Dictionary the word encouragement is defined as:

> "1. The act of encouraging; incitement to action or to practice; 2. That which serves to incite, support, promote, or advance, as favor, countenance, reward, etc.; incentive; increase of confidence."

Here are **11 scriptural facts about encouragement**.

#1 - The best place to find your own personal source of encouragement is the Word of God.

Romans 15:4 in the New Living Translation says:

> "Such things were written in the Scriptures long ago to teach us. And the Scriptures give us hope and encouragement as we wait patiently for God's promises to be fulfilled."

#2 - We have a scriptural responsibility to encourage one another.

1 Thessalonians 2:11 in The Amplified Bible says:

> *"For you know how, as a father [dealing with] his children, we used to exhort each of you personally, stimulating and encouraging and charging you."*

#3 - The encouragement of the Holy Spirit always leads to personal and church growth.

Acts 9:31 in the New Living Translation says:

> *"The church then had peace throughout Judea, Galilee, and Samaria, and it became stronger as the believers lived in the fear of the Lord. And with the encouragement of the Holy Spirit, it also grew in numbers."*

#4 - During times of great persecution the elders of the church understood the need for encouragement for the people.

Acts 13:15 in the New Living Translation says:

> *"After the usual readings from the books of Moses and the prophets, those in charge of the service sent them this message: 'Brothers, if you have any word of encouragement for the people, come and give it.'"*

#5 - Any time believers are together they should be encouraging themselves in the Word and their faith.

Romans 15:32 in the New Living Translation says:

> "Then, by the will of God, I will be able to come to you with a joyful heart, and we will be an encouragement to each other."

#6 - Everything you speak should be for the spiritual progress and encouragement of others.

Ephesians 4:29 in the New Living Translation says:

> "Don't use foul or abusive language. Let everything you say be good and helpful, so that your words will be an encouragement to those who hear them."

#7 - Always be ready to give encouragement in the Lord.

Philemon 1:20 says:

> "Yes, my brother, please do me this favor for the Lord's sake. Give me this encouragement in Christ."

#8 - Everywhere you go ... everyone you speak with ... always bring an encouraging word from the Lord.

Acts 20:1 in The Message Bible says:

> "[Macedonia and Greece] With things back to normal, Paul called the disciples together and

encouraged them to keep up the good work in Ephesus. Then, saying his good-byes, he left for Macedonia. Traveling through the country, passing from one gathering to another, he gave constant encouragement, lifting their spirits and charging them with fresh hope."

#9 - Regardless of what you're facing ... an encouraging word always makes a difference.

Proverbs 12:25 in The Amplified Bible says:

"Anxiety in a man's heart weighs it down, but an encouraging word makes it glad."

#10 - People who encourage others are blessed and appreciated.

1 Corinthians 16:18 in the New Living Translation says:

"They have been a wonderful encouragement to me, as they have been to you. You must show your appreciation to all who serve so well."

#11 – Your encouragement is based in God ... not in humanity.

1 Samuel 30:6 says:

"And David was greatly distressed; for the people spake of stoning him, because the soul of all the people was grieved, every man for his sons

and for his daughters: but David encouraged himself in the LORD his God."

David and his men returned home from battle to find their families had been kidnapped, their valuable possessions stolen and everything else burned to the ground.

Needless to say, *he wasn't having a good day but then things went from bad to worse. His men were now talking of stoning him to death. For there to exist that kind of anger against David, their leader, you know things had to be pretty bad.*

In the midst of such adversity and personal grief ... *David knew there was only one thing to do ... one thing to make him feel better ... one thing to sharpen his perspective ... one thing to bring victory in a desperate, distressing and depressing situation* ... he knew it was time to encourage himself in the Lord by speaking what he knew to be true in God's promises.

When you're going through hell ... the only source of peace and deliverance is through *encouraging yourself in the One who can turn things around* ... just like that.

So here's the question ... when was the last time you encouraged yourself?

What's the best way to encourage yourself?

Reading the *right books* is important.

Making the *right confessions* is very helpful.

Memorizing the *right quotations that will stir your faith* is very good.

Listening to the *right CDs and MP3s* will empower you.

When was the last time *someone encouraged you* ... how did you feel? Did it make you HAPPY HAPPY HAPPY?

When was last time *you encouraged someone* ... how did that make you feel? HAPPY HAPPY HAPPY!

RichThoughts for Breakfast Volume 9

That's a Slap in the Lord's Face

Do you feel misunderstood?

Do you feel there isn't anybody *who understands you?*

Do you disapprove of how your look?

Do you stay within your comfort zone … *because of how you view yourself?*

If you answered "yes" to any of the above questions … then I need to introduce you to my Image Consultant … as **He has a unique way of looking at and dealing with people.**

Here are two quotes that underscore your need for a makeover by an Image Consultant.

"People act like the person they conceive themselves to be." Dr. Maxwell Maltz

"A person cannot consistently perform in a manner which is inconsistent with the way they see themselves." Zig Ziglar

Now here are *seven things my Image Consultant wants you to know.*

1.   You were created in His image.

Genesis 1:26 says:

> *"And God said, Let us make man in our image, after our likeness: and let them have dominion over the fish of the sea, and over the fowl of the air, and over the cattle, and over all the earth, and over every creeping thing that creepeth upon the earth."*

You were created to be the master of the universe. The Living Bible translation of Genesis 1:26 says:

> *"Then God said, "Let us make a man—someone like ourselves, to be the master of all life upon the earth and in the skies and in the seas."*

2.   God has and is continually proving His love for us.

One of the ways to prove you love someone is to give them something precious ... *which may or may not be expensive.*

The uniqueness of the gift ... *whether or not it cost the giver anything* ... **determines, in many cases, the true value of the gift.**

John 3:16 in the Amplified Bible says:

> "For God so greatly loved and dearly prized the world that He [even] gave up His only begotten (unique) Son, so that whoever believes in (trusts in, clings to, relies on) Him shall not perish (come to destruction, be lost) but have eternal (everlasting) life."

God loved you and I so much ... that He gave ... *the thing most valuable to Him.* A gift unlike any other.

Romans 5:8 in the Amplified Bible says:

> "But God shows and clearly proves His [own] love for us by the fact that while we were still sinners, Christ (the Messiah, the Anointed One) died for us."

Now that's what you call real love.

3. You're one of His kids.

Your Heavenly Father can defeat every foe. *You are one of His kids ... never take that for granted or treat it lightly.* I could cite numerous verses but I'm only going to give you two ... both from 1 John.

1 John 3:1-2 in the Amplified Bible says:

> "SEE WHAT [an incredible] quality of love the Father has given (shown, bestowed on) us, that we should [be permitted to] be named and called

and counted the children of God! And so we are! ... but we know that when He comes and is manifested, we shall [as God's children] resemble and be like Him, for we shall see Him just as He [really] is."

1 John 5:1 in the Amplified Bible says:

"EVERYONE WHO believes (adheres to, trusts, and relies on the fact) that Jesus is the Christ (the Messiah) is a born-again child of God; and everyone who loves the Father also loves the one born of Him (His offspring)."

4. **God has plans for you.**

Jeremiah 29:11-13 in the New International Version says:

"For I know the plans I have for you," declares the LORD, "plans to prosper you and not to harm you, plans to give you hope and a future. Then you will call upon me and come and pray to me, and I will listen to you. You will seek me and find me when you seek me with all your heart."

I remember the very first time I ever read **"For I know the plans I have for you."** It was in my Thompson Chain Reference Bible.

My spirit leapt ... because for the very first time **I fully realized that God had plans for Harold Herring.**

I want you to take a moment and realize that God has plans for you.

In fact, I encourage you to **personalize the phrase**.

The Contemporary English Version of Jeremiah 29:11 says:

> *"I will bless you with a future filled with hope--a future of success, not of suffering."*

The Word of God says:

> *"I **will** bless (Your Name) with a future filled with hope—a future of success, not of suffering."*

5.   God provides for every need you have.

Let's look at three verses in Philippians 4.

Philippians 4:6 in The Living Bible says:

> *"Don't worry about anything; instead, pray about everything; tell God your needs, and don't forget to thank him for his answers."*

When we commune with our Heavenly Father ... He always ... *always provides for and empowers us to achievements* **beyond our natural mind and/or abilities.**

Philippians 4:13 in The Living Bible says:

"For I can do everything God asks me to with the help of Christ who gives me the strength and power."

Philippians 4:19 in the New Living Translation says:

"And this same God who takes care of me will supply all your needs from his glorious riches, which have been given to us in Christ Jesus."

6. **God never wants you to feel unloved and unappreciated.**

I'm going to read Ephesians 1:3-6 in the Message Bible where we find seven reasons why God wants you to feel loved, appreciate and highly valued.

"How blessed is God! And what a blessing he is! He's the Father of our Master, Jesus Christ, and <u>takes us to the high places of blessing in him</u>. Long <u>before he laid down earth's foundations, he had us in mind</u>, had <u>settled on us as the focus of his love, to be made whole and holy by his love</u>. Long, long ago <u>he decided to adopt us into his family through Jesus Christ. (What pleasure he took in planning this</u>!) He wanted us to enter <u>into the celebration of his lavish gift-giving</u> by the hand of his beloved Son."

7. **God will not condemn what He created.**

Romans 8:1 in the Amplified Bible says:

> "THEREFORE, [there is] now no condemnation (no adjudging guilty of wrong) for those who are in Christ Jesus, who live [and] walk not after the dictates of the flesh, but after the dictates of the Spirit."

God chose not to condemn us to an eternity of damnation ... *but rather He gave us a choice of the abundant and eternal life.*

Let me ask you a question ...

<u>If God isn't going to condemn you ... do you really think anybody else should have the right to</u>? Absolutely not!

Now that we understand how our Image Consultant views us ... we need to consider several other things.

We need to recognize that we can improve our self-image.

These two verses are confirmation of your ability to change how you view yourself.

Ephesians 4:24 in the Amplified Bible says:

> "And put on the new nature (the regenerate self) created in God's image, [Godlike] in true righteousness and holiness."

Colossians 3:10 in the Amplified Bible says:

> "And have clothed yourselves with the new [spiritual self], which is [ever in the process of being] renewed and remolded into [fuller and more perfect knowledge upon] knowledge after the image (the likeness) of Him Who created it."

We should never confuse *who we are with what we can do ... or what we've done*.

First, create a written list of what you've done so far in your life.

Second, create a list of your strengths and weaknesses.

Write down how to maximize the former and minimize the latter. And pay more attention to your strengths ... and the weaknesses will not hinder you.

Third, improve your self-image by increasing your skills. Get involved in a structured personal growth and developmental program ... otherwise known as renewing your mind. You can find *Spiritual Entrepreneur: 21 Day Information for Success* on my website at www.HaroldHerring.com.

Fourth, create a positive confession about your self-image ... speaking only the pure, the powerful and/or the positive over your life ... or when talking to yourself or in describing yourself to others.

Fifth and finally, never ever say ... you have a poor self-image. Actually, that's a slap in the face of our Lord ... because we are made in His image and after His likeness and there's nothing poor about that.

Think about it.

7 Reasons to Know Where You're At

Here are 7 reasons to know where you're at ... **to get where you're going.**

1.   You've Got to Know Where You're At.

When it comes to your money ... if you don't know where you're at ... then you'll never know where you're going ... in fact, you'll end up where the creditors want you to be.

Proverbs 27:23 tells us:

> *"Be thou diligent to know the state of thy flocks, and look well to thy herds."*

In the Old Testament, *wealth was often measured by the size of a person's flock or herd.* It was critical for a person to know not only the location of every animal *but also its physical condition.*

In the agrarian society that dominated the Old Testament world ... **the location and state of a person's**

flocks was critical to wealth increase.

Now it's time for you to get out your checkbook and all your bills. *You need to know the state of your flock … what you have at the moment.*

Any increase in wealth begins with an honest assessment of what you've got and where you're at.

Do you know your checkbook balance?

Do you know exactly *how much you owe every single creditor you've got?*

Do you know how much money you make and where it goes?

Do you know the balance, interest rate, monthly payment and remaining months on every single debt you owe?

Do you have a plan to pay all these bills off rapidly?

If you can't answer "yes" to the five questions above, then chances are you're not looking after your "flocks and herds" the way the Bible indicates you should.

It's important … **no, it's absolutely necessary for you to know EVERYTHING about your finances** … to know the state of your flocks and herds *if you want to break free from the bondage of debt into God's glorious provision for your life.*

It's your time to take action ... delay will only cost you money.

2. You've Got to Know Where You're Going.

Once you determine where you're at ... then you can more accurately know the direction and location in which you're heading.

It's very important to understand that **it's not where you're at ... it's where you're going**.

Your destination is your goal.

If you goal is to be a millionaire ... you have an empty goal. **Becoming a millionaire is serendipity to fulfilling your vision, your dreams and your goals.**

Stephen Covey in his book *The Seven Habits of Highly Effective People* defines the *second habit this way:*

"Begin with the end in mind."

It's important to always keep the end in mind ... *never lose sight of your destination.*

It might surprise you to know that many Christians ... *not only don't know where they are in life ... they don't have a clue where they want to be.*

When you ask God ... He will answer your questions about direction and your purpose for being here on planet earth ... *then you will know your destination.*

3.   You've Got to Take the First Step Toward Your Destination.

If you don't like the way your world is at the moment, *change it.*

You have the God-given ability to change your life ... your direction ... your destiny ... one step at a time.

Write it out.

I have the God-given ability to change my life ... my direction ... my destiny ... one step at a time ... starting today.

A Chinese philosopher once said:

> "The journey of a thousand miles begins with the first step."

The Word of God reveals in Psalm 111:10 in the Contemporary English Version what that first step should be. The scripture says:

> "Respect and obey the LORD! This is the first step to wisdom and good sense. God will always be respected."

From the very first step of your journey ... your focus needs to be obedience to His direction.

<u>Be wise to every trick of the enemy as he seeks to</u>

slow your progress ... change your direction and get your eyes off your ultimate destination.

4.   **You've Got to Endure Those Traveling in a Direction Different than the Path You're On.**

In life there will be people ... even those close to you, including family members *who will not share your dream or the pursuit of excellence in your life.* **They just want to go with the flow** *while you're determined to travel/swim upstream.*

If you've ever noticed a river ... the easiest thing to do is float downstream. It doesn't take any effort ... any planning ... it just seems to happen.

It's important to *check out what's floating downstream with you ... broken and or rotten tree limbs ... anything dead ... anything or anyone just along for the ride.*

God didn't call you just to come along for the ride. *He called you to excel at what you're doing ...* He called you to be a difference maker ... *a destiny shaper.*

The path of least resistance will lead you to a place you don't want to be.

5.   **You've Got to Walk on By Those Who Are Slowing Up Your Journey.**

Do your friends encourage, discourage and/or ignore your dreams, hopes and plans for the future?

<u>You need no one around you who is holding you back from the progress that you should be making.</u>

Job 12:4 in the New Living Translation says:

> "Yet my friends laugh at me, for I call on God and expect an answer. I am a just and blameless man, yet they laugh at me."

Make no mistake ... if your friends are talking about and laughing at others ... *when they're not around* **... they will be making fun of you when you're not around.**

If you're friends aren't empowering and encouraging you on your journey to success ... you need to find friends who will.

6.   You've Got to Focus on the Details.

If the devil can break your focus on what's necessary for success ... *then he has disrupted and delayed* ... if not destroyed ... your destiny.

If you've ever wondered how God feels about attention to details being fundamental to your success ... I suggest you read 2 Corinthians 6:1-3 in the Message Bible very carefully. It says:

> "Companions as we are in this work with you, we beg you, please don't squander one bit of this marvelous life God has given us. God reminds us, I heard your call in the nick of time;

The day you needed me, I was there to help. Well, now is the right time to listen, the day to be helped. Don't put it off; don't frustrate God's work by showing up late, throwing a question mark over everything we're doing. **Our work as God's servants gets validated—or not—in the details ..."**

Make no mistake ... God wants you paying attention to the details ... while the enemy wants you to ignore them.

7. You've Got to Know Where You're At ... When You Get There.

One of our daughters ... I won't say which one ... has been bewildered by directions on more than one occasion.

At one time she was directionally challenged by any map even with the best MapQuest Directions and an onboard navigator (traveling companion.)

Praise God for the invention of the GPS.

The GPS allows you to know where you're at ... at any given moment and whether or not you're heading in the right direction. Not only that ... *it will tell you when you will arrive and if you need to alter your current directions.*

As believers we need to activate our spiritual GPS. **We must continually monitor our progress in our** journey to success and financial freedom.

Truthfully, our progress should be clearly evident to others as well.

1 Timothy 4:15 in the New International Version says:

> *"Give your complete attention to these matters. Throw yourself into your tasks so that everyone will see your progress."*

Your journey to your destination ... *can and should be an inspiration to others.*

What I'm about to say ... may at first glance seem ironic ... however, please know the greatest compliment anyone could ever pay you is to say ... **"If you can do it ... I know I can too."**

Your success in life should be duplicatable ... others need to know they can find success by finding and following the red dot.

Day 7

7 Things We Can Expect from God

I begin each day filled with supernatural expectation about the manifestation of God's *presence*, power, *provision*, protection, *promotion*, peace and *promises*.

As I was writing those words **something ignited in my spirit and I knew** <u>God had just given me the seven things we can expect to receive from Him</u>.

1. Presence

The best place for you to be ... is *not in the Presidential Suite of a four-star hotel ... the Lincoln Bedroom at the White House ... the luxury suite of a cruise ship sailing through the Mediterranean Sea* ... even though all those places are nice ... <u>the best place for a believer to be</u> *is in God's Presence*.

As a born-again believer you have the privilege of access into His presence. That is something that we shouldn't *and can't take for granted*. It is beyond awesome if you think about it.

Psalm 118:20 in the New Living Translation says:

> "These gates lead to the presence of the Lord, and the godly enter there."

Not only can you enter into His presence ... but *He even tells you the best time to find Him.*

Proverbs 8:17 says:

> "I love them that love me; and those that seek me early shall find me."

Not only are we to seek His presence early in the morning but *we're to do so with expectation.*

Psalm 5:3 in the New International Version says:

> "In the morning, O Lord, you hear my voice; in the morning I lay my requests before you and wait in expectation."

2. **Peace**

When Jesus left Planet Earth ... He gave us a powerful gift ... found in John 14:27 which says:

> "Peace I leave with you, my peace I give unto you: not as the world giveth, give I unto you. Let not your heart be troubled, neither let it be afraid."

The Lord will give you His strength and peace in

the midst of every adversity.

Psalm 29:11 says:

> "The LORD will give strength unto his people; the LORD will bless his people with peace."

Philippians 4:7 in the New Living Translation says:

> "Then you will experience God's peace, which exceeds anything we can understand. His peace will guard your hearts and minds as you live in Christ Jesus."

3.   **Protection**

God gives us protection from all adversaries beyond anything the world has ever seen ... and it's free.

Psalm 5:11 in the New Living Translation says:

> "But let all who take refuge in you be glad; let them ever sing for joy. Spread your protection over them that those who love your name may rejoice in you."

Not only does God offer you protection ... but your enemies become His enemies.

Exodus 23:22 in the Amplified Bible says:

> "But if you will indeed listen to and obey His voice ... I will be an enemy to your enemies and

an adversary to your adversaries."

Now that's what I call a real home security ... much better than ADT or Brinks.

4. Promises

At least once a week, we are instructed to pause and remember the promises God has made to us.

Exodus 31:16 in The Living Bible says:

> *"Work six days only, for the seventh day is a special day to remind you of my covenant – a weekly reminder forever of my promises to the people of Israel."*

God made certain promises to your spiritual forefathers ... *promises that He will never forget and always honor if we embrace them in our own lives.*

No matter the adversity you may face ... God will never forget or forgo the promises He made to your spiritual relatives.

Deuteronomy 4:31 in The Living Bible says:

> *"For the Lord your God is merciful – he will not abandon you nor destroy you nor forget the promises he has made to your ancestors."*

Never ever get discouraged when you don't see the immediate manifestation of God's promises to

you.

Joshua 21:45 in the New Living Translations says:

> *"Not a single one of all the good promises the LORD had given to the family of Israel was left unfulfilled; everything he had spoken came true."*

5. Power

I'm about to speak a five-word sentence ... *the reality of which can change your life forever.* Here it is: **"God hasn't left you powerless."**

Acts 1:8 says:

> *"... ye shall receive power, after that the Holy Ghost is come upon you ... (then) ye shall become witnesses ..."*

The power Jesus promises after the Holy Ghost comes upon you is *enabling power* (dunamis).

The Greek word *dunamis* means:

"ability."

So let's look at this verse again as I expand the paraphrase for you.

> *"You shall receive the ability after the Holy Ghost has come upon you, and you will be able to witness of me simultaneously in Jerusalem,*

and in Judea, and in Samaria, and to the uttermost parts of the earth."

6. Promotion

Have you ever been promoted?

From one grade to the next in school ... from one level of accomplishment to the next in the Boy or Girl Scouts ... *from one rank to a higher one in the military or from one position to a different one at your place of employment?* Or from owning one store to opening another?

If you think the promotion was a result of your skills and/or your hard work, *then I suggest you read, study and meditate* on Psalm 75:6-8 in the Message Bible:

> *"For promotion and power come from nowhere on earth, but only from God. He promotes one and deposes another."*

Your promotion comes from the Lord. **He gives you the power and favor for advancement in every single area of human endeavor.**

7. Provisions

When you give God your best ... what is most precious to you ... He will give you provisions above and beyond your wildest expectations ... even in the midst of the direst circumstances.

In Genesis 42 through 45, there's a story told about Joseph. It's the second year of the famine and the warehouse in Egypt is full.

One day, Joseph is out on the porch and he sees his brothers ... the very ones who had sold him into slavery. He gives his brothers an audience.

Joseph's brothers don't realize who he is because he looks like an Egyptian, but he knows who they are. *The men are seated at a banquet table having the opportunity to experience riches that are available even in a famine.*

When the whole thing comes to a close at dinner that night, he gets them a few little sacks of corn and they go back home.

Genesis 42:25 says:

> *"Then Joseph commanded to fill their sacks with corn, and to restore every man's money into his sack, and to give them provision for the way: and thus did he unto them."*

Before his brothers leave, Joseph puts them on the spot. *He knows their brother Benjamin is the most precious thing in their daddy's house.*

He makes certain *they know that if they come back and don't bring Benjamin—they won't see his face again. They will be stuck in that line over there with the thousands of others who want grain.* They won't have privileged access to the supply sergeant of the world.

Just to be sure they understand, *Joseph binds his brother Simeon before their eyes and keeps him in Egypt.*

The brothers get home distressed but with some food for now, so the pressure of the famine is taken off them for a season. After a while their food runs out again. Jacob gives his sons some money and says, "Go get us some more food."

They said, *"Daddy, money's not going to do it. He said we have to bring Benjamin also."*

Jacob said, "Why did you tell him about Benjamin? Blabbermouths! What did you have to go tell him about Benjamin for?"

Then they said, *"Daddy, we didn't tell him about Benjamin. He knew about Benjamin. He knew what was precious in our lives."*

Finally, they send Benjamin, and through a series of circumstances, Joseph realizes that the precious is now entrusted to him. *As he reveals himself, they no longer go home with sacks of grain.* They now carry wagonloads of grain. *Everybody in Egypt is eating out of sacks but they're eating out of wagons.*

When we give God our best ... what is precious to us ... then He will release into our stewardship wagonloads of blessings.

Today expect God's presence, power, *provision,* protection, *promotion,* peace and *promises* and I might add His potential and possibilities as well.

7 Ways to Overcome Negative Stuff

Here are seven ways to overcome **negative stuff**.

1.   Talk to yourself.

Despite popular opinion, there is nothing wrong with talking to yourself ... there is nothing wrong with answering yourself ... but if you say "huh" *then you're in trouble.*

You not only need to be talking to yourself ... but you need to be saying the right things which is the Word of God.

You also need to know that if you're not talking to yourself ... somebody else is.

Your choice of words will reveal who you really are ... the scripture says in Matthew 12:34 that *". . . for out of the abundance of the heart the mouth speaketh."*

Matthew 12:34-37 in the Message Bible says:

"How do you suppose what you say is worth

anything when you are so foul-minded? It's your heart, not the dictionary, that gives meaning to your words. A good person produces good deeds and words season after season. An evil person is a blight on the orchard. Let me tell you something: Every one of these careless words is going to come back to haunt you. There will be a time of Reckoning. **Words are powerful; take them seriously.** *Words can be your salvation. Words can also be your damnation."*

Verse 37 says in part, *"Words are powerful; take them seriously,"* especially when they're coming out of your mouth.

2. **Who else should you allow to speak into your life?**

You may need to change who you are allowing to speak into your life. *You wouldn't allow a neighbor to walk into your living room and dump the entire contents of their garbage can into the middle of your floor.*

Yet, <u>way too many believers are allowing their neighbors, friends and family to dump negative thinking and harmful conversation into the middle of their mental living room</u>.

Dr. Mike Murdock, biblical teacher and our close friend and mentor, says that *he can tell your future once he determines who you're listening to.*

Your success in life ... will be determined by

whose voice you listen to.

There is only one voice that gets you absolutely accurate information and direction every time.

Galatians 5:16 in the New Living Translation says:

> "So I say, let the Holy Spirit guide your lives. Then you won't be doing what your sinful nature craves."

3.   Participate in activities that you enjoy.

Every sporting event ... *every television show has a break in the action.* You need to plan and participate in things that relax you physically and mentally.

Everyone ... and that includes you and especially me ... *needs to decompress from the pressures of life* or, if you prefer, *the toils of the day.*

Start your relaxation and recreational time right where you are. It may be as simple as sitting out on the porch during the summertime and *watching the sun set.* In the winter, it might be building a snow man.

It could also be a walk in the park ... swimming at a public pool ... going for a walk on your street. I don't need to make the list for you ... get a sheet of paper and *create your own list of activities that you'd enjoy doing ... without messing up your budget.*

## 4.	Do not allow anybody including the enemy to direct your focus at will.

This key is close to number two but there is a difference. Find a quiet time and secret place where you can spend quality time with the Lord.

Give your highest priority to reading the word. Don't allow the television set or the desire to surf the net to interfere with your devotional time.

<u>**I can tell you the enemy will try to break your focus on the Lord.**</u> It might be a baby crying … a child needing help with homework … The point is to continue to go back. God know when your baby cries or another need arises … just continue to keep Him your focus.

<u>**There is nothing more valuable than your time with God.**</u> Guard it diligently.

## 5.	Create confessions that energize your faith.

First, your confession should be based on your speaking right words. What are the right words? Simple answer—the words in the scriptures.

Ephesians 4:29 in the Amplified Bible says:

> "Let no foul or polluting language, nor evil word nor unwholesome or worthless talk [ever] come out of your mouth, but only such [speech] as is good and beneficial to the spiritual progress of

others, as is fitting to the need and the occasion, that it may be a blessing and give grace (God's favor) to those who hear it."

Second, you can change where you are in life by what comes out of your mouth.

Create your confession based on what you want to see manifested ... as long as it's based on the Word of God.

Third, make your confession for at least twenty-one days. Studies show any action taken daily for twenty-one days will very likely become a habit. The habits we form become the lifestyles we create and live by.

If you don't own *Spiritual Entrepreneur: A 21-Day Information System for Success,* order it today from our website at www.HaroldHerring.com.

Fourth, your circumstances should never alter your confession.

Fifth, speak your confession every day. Your confession will directly impact your expectation which determines your manifestation.

6.   Consume the right kind of mental food.

If you want to replace the negativity in your life ... then you need to be feeding on the right stuff. There is an old saying that what you feed grows and what you starve dies.

The right stuff is to turn off sports or political talk radio or the music stations and listen to teaching CDs instead.

Listen to your pastor's sermon from last Sunday, or a professional development teaching series or any of the absolutely fantastic teaching CDs from the Debt Free Army (smiling). Educate and empower yourself while you drive.

A few days back, I discussed creating a university on wheels.

If you commute more than 30 minutes a day ... five days a week ... whether it's to work or on errands ... that's 150 minutes a week ... 7,800 minutes a year or a total of <u>130 hours per year in your daily drive ... which equals over 16 work days a year</u>.

This will allow you to manifest the Law of Displacement in your life. You will be removing the garbage others placed in your mind with the *pure*, the *powerful* and the *positive* from the Word of God.

I'm reminded of a quote by Albert Einstein that I dearly love.

"If you feed your mind as often as you feed your stomach, then you'll never have to worry about feeding your stomach or a roof over your head or clothes on your back."

Success will never come to you ... unless you're willing to change your attitude ... which will change by what you feed your mind.

It's also important to understand that success will never manifest around you until it's established within you.

7. Reach out and touch someone.

Ephesians 6:8 in the New Living Translation says:

> *"Remember that the Lord will reward each one of us for the good we do ..."*

We're admonished throughout the scriptures to develop a heart of compassion ... to love others with the love of God.

2 Peter 1:7 in the Amplified Bible says:

> *"And in [exercising] godliness [develop] brotherly affection, and in [exercising] brotherly affection [develop] Christian love."*

The good news is that developing and displaying Christian love brings its own reward.

2 Peter 1:8 in the New Living Translation says:

> *"The more you grow like this, the more productive and useful you will be in your knowledge of our Lord Jesus Christ."*

And one final thing ... look for the best in others ... even if they aren't looking for the best in themselves.

1 Thessalonians 5:13 in the Message Bible says:

> *"... Look for the best in each other, and always do your best to bring it out."*

If you look for the best in everybody else ... it will take the worst out of you.

RichThoughts for Breakfast Volume 9

How to Be Well-Pleasing to God

Who do you want to please ... your spouse, mother, father, sister, brother, best friend, neighbors, pastor, employer *or most anybody you meet?*

Truthfully, there is only one person that you ever need to worry about pleasing ... because *if He's happy happy happy and well pleased, you can find contentment and success in life.*

What does well-pleasing to God really mean ...

Well-pleasing according to Strong's Concordance is the Greek word (G2101) which comes from two Greek root words. The first root word is (G2095) and it means:

"well-off, fare well, prosper."

That same Greek word is used in Matthew 25:21 which says:

> "His lord said unto him, Well done, thou good and faithful servant: thou hast been faithful over

a few things, I will make thee ruler over many things: enter thou into the joy of thy lord."

And the second root word comes from Strong's (G701) which means:

"pleasing, agreeable."

John 8:29 says:

"And he that sent me is with me: the Father hath not left me alone; <u>for I do always those things that please him</u>."

The Message Bible translation of John 8:29 says:

"The One who sent me stays with me. He doesn't abandon me. He sees how much joy I take in pleasing him."

The scripture offers some very basic guidelines on how you can live a life that is well-pleasing to God.

Matthew 11:26 in the New American Standard says:

"For this way was well-pleasing to God."

1.   Living your life under authority is well-pleasing to God.

Titus 2:9 in the New American Standard version says:

"Urge bondslaves to be subject to their own

masters in everything, to be well-pleasing, not argumentative."

The New King James Version says *"not answering back is well pleasing to God."*

Lucifer rejected Heavenly authority ... he created strife and confusion by failing to recognize God's authority. *He is still creating problems by deceptively blurring lines of authority.* He does this in the workplace, in churches and in homes.

And frankly, he uses television and movies to blur the lines.

Colossians 3:20 in the New American Standard says:

"Children, be obedient to your parents in all things, for this is well pleasing to the Lord."

This may seem insignificant ... but a rebellious people will NEVER prosper and achieve the quality of life that God envisions for them.

One more thing on authority. It's easy to be under authority when things are going well ... but the real measure of your obedience to authority comes when you disagree with those over you.

1 Peter 2:13-17 in the Message Bible says:

"**Make the Master proud of you by being good citizens.** Respect the authorities, what-

ever their level; they are God's emissaries for keeping order. It is God's will that by doing good, you might cure the ignorance of the fools who think you're a danger to society. Exercise your freedom by serving God, not by breaking the rules. <u>Treat everyone you meet with dignity</u>. Love your spiritual family. Revere God. Respect the government."

We cannot account for what anyone else does, but we will give an account for everything we think, say and do. Understand this ... authority is important to God.

2.   Living the right kind of life is well-pleasing to God.

Romans 12:1 in the Amplified Bible says:

"I APPEAL to you therefore, brethren, and beg of you in view of [all] the mercies of God, to make a decisive dedication of your bodies [presenting all your members and faculties] as a living sacrifice, holy (devoted, consecrated) and well pleasing to God, which is your reasonable (rational, intelligent) service and spiritual worship."

I love the way the Amplified says make a "decisive dedication" in Romans 12. *That's the kind of commitment God wants from us.* I can assure you that He's not going to listen to excuses about why we didn't fulfill our divine purpose or maximize our time.

In fact, on Judgment Day, as He reviews the things in our Book of Life, He is probably going to ask us a question with seven words.

"Did you do the best you could have done?"

God is the Creator of the Universe, the Alpha and the Omega and He has even numbered the hairs on your head ... *so He will already know whether what you've done is your best or not.*

So here's the question, in your workplace environment, have you made a decisive dedication to excellence? *Are you totally committed to quality in everything your hands find to do? Have you decided to never settle for less than the best?*

God wants to bless you beyond measure ... but you must live a life that's well-pleasing to Him.

2 Corinthians 5:9 in the New King James Version says:

> "Therefore we make it our aim, whether present or absent, to be well pleasing to Him."

3. Your offerings should be well-pleasing to Him.

Philippians 4:18 in the New American Standard says:

> "But I have received everything in full and have an abundance; I am amply supplied, having re-

ceived from Epaphroditus what you have sent, a fragrant aroma, an acceptable sacrifice, well-pleasing to God."

What is an offering that is well-pleasing to God?

It's simple: the one He tells you to give.

Whether what you give is big or small in your own eyes, *the important thing to remember is to listen to the voice of the Lord and obey Him in the offering. Way too many believers are tipping God ... because they think* that's what they can afford to sow or what they've always given. Ask God. Only He knows what you need to reap down the road.

I challenge you to think very carefully about the three points I'm going to share with you *about giving an offering that is well-pleasing to God.*

First, God watches you give.

Mark 12:42 says:

> *"And Jesus sat over against the treasury, and beheld how the people cast money into the treasury ..."*

Jesus pulled a chair over where He could get a good view of how much people gave.

Second, He watches how much you give.

Mark 12:41-42 says:

> "And Jesus sat over against the treasury, and beheld how the people cast money into the treasury: and many that were rich cast in much. And there came a certain poor widow, and she threw in two mites, which make a farthing."

God does not tell you to give based on what's in your wallet, pocketbook or checking account ... but He does watch how much you give.

Third, God brags about givers.

Mark 12:43-44 says:

> "And he called unto him his disciples, and saith unto them, Verily I say unto you, That this poor widow hath cast more in, than all they which have cast into the treasury: For all they did cast in of their abundance; but she of her want did cast in all that she had, even all her living."

This poor widow did not give what was convenient or usual ... the scripture says that she cast in all ... everything she had ... not just the chump change ... but "all her living."

No doubt, on that day, Jesus observed some folks making large gifts to the treasury ... but *He only recognized and praised the one who gave all she had.*

The one who overlooked every circumstance in her

life ... *who rejected all rationalization and justification for not giving* ... the scripture memorializes the poor widow who gave all she had.

Final Word

If you want to have a life worth living ... a life well-pleasing to God, then make your offerings sweet and acceptable in His sight.

We need to also heed the words found in Ephesians 5:10 in the Young's Literal Translation:

> *"In your daily life make sure you're doing what is well-pleasing to the Lord."*

Make no mistake. Hebrews 13:21 in the New King James Version says God wants to *"make you complete in every good work to do His will, working in you what is well pleasing in His sight, through Jesus Christ, to whom be glory forever and ever. Amen."*

Our goal ... our life's purpose ... should be to be well-pleasing in His sight and that will make our Heavenly Father ... HAPPY HAPPY HAPPY.

Day 10

You've Got What They've Got

What do you have in common with the President or any member of Congress?

What do you have in common with any actor or actress?

What do you have in common with Robert Kiyosaki, the author of *Rich Dad, Poor Dad*?

What do you have in common with your youngest child or grandchild?

What do you have in common with Creflo Dollar, Kenneth Copeland or Joyce Meyer?

What do you have in common with the wino curled up in a pasteboard box on a rainy day?

What do you have in common with a convicted felon?

What do you have in common with any and everybody who is drawing a breath at this very moment?

The answer is *time* ... it is our greatest treasure here on Earth.

Yes, you've got what ... they've got ... time.

Early this morning and I do mean early ... I was directed by the Lord to teach on time.

Mention time, and most people immediately think, "I need to manage my time better."

You no longer have to worry about managing time. *Time is constant.* There are sixty seconds in a minute, sixty minutes in an hour, twenty-four hours in a day, seven days in a week, and fifty-two weeks in a year.

Time never changes. **However, we must learn to manage *ourselves*.**

Time never changes but **the very good news is ... we can**.

Please understand, this *is not a time management lesson* to help you become more effective for your employer or even your family.

You *must first become more effective for the Kingdom of God. If believers will learn to be effective for the Kingdom, they will automatically be effective for their families and their employers.*

The greatest treasure and the most precious commodity God has entrusted to you is your time.

Everything you do takes time. *There are many things you can get along without;* however, you cannot get along without time.

A proper relationship with Jesus Christ will make proper time management possible.

Proverbs 10:27 in The Living Bible says, *"Reverence for God adds hours to each day ..."*

Think about that long enough to let it sink in!

As always, whenever there is something of value, *there will be robbers trying to steal it. Your time is one of your treasures.* It is important that you *clearly identify anything that tries to steal your time.* If you don't, many random things will cause you to become an unfaithful steward.

Carefully consider the following 26 time bandits.

1) Procrastination
2) *Poor communication*
3) Waiting
4) *Overload*
5) Poor sense of time frames
6) *Unclear goals and priorities*
7) Failure to delegate
8) *Blame shifting*
9) Unnecessary or poorly planned committee meetings
10) *Excessive television viewing*
11) Misuse of the cell phone

12) *Uncontrolled interruptions*
13) Not being able to say "no"
14) *Internet surfing*
15) Poor habits
16) *Excessive paperwork*
17) Worry
18) *Guilt*
19) Frivolous reading
20) *Sleeping late*
21) Fixation with social networking
22) *Carefully reading junk mail*
23) Arguing
24) *Unimportant comparisons*
25) Not concentrating when important instructions are being given
26) *Poor planning or scheduling*

Go back over these and underline the time bandits that are robbing you. *Now, make up your mind that they are on your drop list. They must be removed if you ever want to hear, "Well done, thou good and faithful steward," from your Heavenly Father.*

Before we go any further ... I think it's important to get a clearer understanding of Proverbs 6:21:

> *"For where your treasure is, there will your heart be also."*

WEBSTER'S NEW INTERCOLLEGIATE DICTIONARY defines *treasure* as: **"money, jewels or precious metals stored up."** It is also defined as **"something of great worth or value to you."**

For where there is something of great worth or value to you, "there your heart will be also."

What is of great worth or value to you? *We've already established that your time is your greatest treasure.*

Next, you need to understand what it means when the *scripture says your heart will go where your treasure goes.*

If your treasure is in a new car, new boat, or new set of golf clubs, that's where your heart will be.

Wherever your heart is, that's where you will find "whatever is of worth or value to you."

You might say, "But my heart is with the Lord!"

Well, here's the question. *Is there enough evidence to prove your statement?* If your relationship with God is where your treasure is, *how much time are you spending with Him?* How much of your money goes into what is important to Him?

To find out—first, examine your time.

Let's look at how an average person spends 24 hours.

Typically six to eight hours a day are spent sleeping.

This leaves 16-18 hours.

Another 8 hours are used up working.

Now 8-10 hours remain in the day.

One hour is spent dressing/undressing, which leaves 7-9.

One and a half hours are concerned with eating which brings the number down to 5 ½-7 ½.

Lastly, 1 hour is typically spent commuting per day.

That leaves 4 ½ - 6 ½ hours a day. *The average person in this country spends four hours every day watching television.* That leaves ½- 2 ½ hours for the internet or other things that are important to you.

Do you know where that time goes or does it just slip away? Where are you spending your time?

Scientists tell us that we have about 10,000 thoughts each day. *How many of those thoughts (416 per hour) are directed toward the things of God?*

What does the Bible have to say about time?

Romans 13:11-12 in the King James Version says:

> *"... knowing the time, that now it is high time to awake out of sleep: for now is our salvation nearer than when we believed. The night is far spent, the day is at hand: let us therefore cast off the works of darkness, and let us put on the armour of light."*

Colossians 4:5 in the Amplified Bible says:

> "Behave yourselves wisely (living prudently and with discretion) in your relations with those of the outside world ... making the very most of the time and seizing (buying up) the opportunity."

Joshua 1:8 in the King James Version says:

> "This book of the law shall not depart out of thy mouth; but thou shalt meditate therein day and night, that thou mayest observe to do according to all that is written therein: for then though shalt make thy way prosperous, and then thou shalt have good success."

To meditate on the Word day and night, you must control what you allow to come into your mind. <u>If you keep your mind focused on Him, you will be a strong tree, producing good fruit.</u>

If your spouse is of worth or value to you, *are you spending time together?* Are you spending it with your children?

Are you investing treasure into your family?

Colossians 3:2 tells us:

> "Set your affection on things above, not on things on the earth."

I think by now you understand that <u>your time is your</u>

<u>life</u>.

It's "time" to determine who's in control of your life. Either you will manage your time, or it will manage to control you.

Let me close with the words of Romans 13:11-14 in the Message Bible which says:

> *"But make sure that you don't get so absorbed and exhausted in taking care of all your day-by-day obligations that you lose track of the time and doze off, oblivious to God. The night is about over, dawn is about to break. Be up and awake to what God is doing! God is putting the finishing touches on the salvation work he began when we first believed. We can't afford to waste a minute, must not squander these precious daylight hours in frivolity and indulgence, in sleeping around and dissipation, in bickering and grabbing everything in sight. Get out of bed and get dressed! Don't loiter and linger, waiting until the very last minute. Dress yourselves in Christ, and be up and about!"*

Day 11

7 Ways to Hush Your Circumstances

Mark 4:39 says:

"And he arose, and rebuked the wind, and said unto the sea, Peace, be still. And the wind ceased, and there was a great calm."

Here are seven ways to hush your circumstances or quiet the storms of life.

1.   When trouble is headed your way ... always do what Jesus did.

When the storms of life rise up against you ... be at peace.

When troubles come your way ... do you find yourself having sleepless nights? Tossing and turning ... worrying about what may or may not happen?

Don't you think Jesus knew there was a storm forming ... about to churn into a dangerous storm? We should follow His direction as found in the Contemporary English Version of Mark 4:38 which says:

"Jesus was in the back of the boat with his head on a pillow, and he was asleep."

Matthew 6:34 in the Message Bible offers some great advice when it says:

"Give your entire attention to what God is doing right now, and don't get worked up about what may or may not happen tomorrow. God will help you deal with whatever hard things come up when the time comes."

2. He will never tell you to do anything dangerous without a way of escape.

Mark 4:35 in the Amplified Bible says:

"On that same day [when] evening had come, He said to them, Let us go over to the other side [of the lake]."

Did you believe the Son of God knew what was going to happen ... before it ever happened?

Acts 2:23 in the New Living Translation says:

"But God knew what would happen, and his pre-arranged plan was carried out when Jesus was betrayed. With the help of lawless Gentiles, you nailed him to a cross and killed him."

If He knew He was going to be betrayed and crucified ... He most certainly knew about a storm in the Sea of

Galilee.

Since Jesus knew the storm was coming ... do you really think He would have put the disciples ... those closest to Him ... in a position to drown and die? Of course not!

In everything you face in life ... *no matter how great the temptation or seemingly insurmountable the problem may be* ... God always provides a way of escape.

3.   **God is not moved by your circumstances ... and neither should you be.**

Let me give you an absolute fact ... if you're doing what God has called you to do ... fulfilling His vision for your life ... being obedient to His divine direction ... stuff is going to happen.

I remember an airline flight ... where there was a violent thunderstorm in the distance as the plane leveled off at its cruising altitude. As we drew closer and closer to the thunderstorm ... the lady sitting next to me ... became increasingly nervous and fearful about the storm.

I listened quietly until she said ... she didn't want to die in a plane crash. I confidently told her that our plane was not going to crash ... that we were going to arrive safely at our destination.

When she asked me how I could be so sure ... I said: "Because I'm on this plane and God still has a lot for me to accomplish in my life." Then I told her that He had plans for her as well.

That's when I discovered she was a strong Christian ... but her faith was weakened because of facing fear.

She had forgotten the lesson of faith.

Isaiah 41:10 in the Message Bible says:

> *"Don't panic. I'm with you. There's no need to fear for I'm your God. I'll give you strength. I'll help you. I'll hold you steady, keep a firm grip on you."*

4.   When in the midst of the storms of life ... call on Him and quote the Word.

Psalm 86:5-7 says:

> *"In the day of my trouble I will call upon thee: for thou wilt answer me."*

If you need the peace of God in your life ... if you need deliverance from the storms of adversity ... heed the words of Jeremiah 29:12-14 in the Amplified Bible which says:

> *"Then you will call upon Me, and you will come and pray to Me, and I will hear and heed you. Then you will seek Me, inquire for, and require Me [as a vital necessity] and find Me when you search for Me with all your heart. I will be found*

by you, says the Lord, and I will release you from captivity ..."

5. When you rely on the Word ... all your fears will leave.

The best reason not to be afraid ... is because the Word of God tells you not to.

Isaiah 41:10 in the Contemporary English Version says:

> *"Don't be afraid. I am with you. Don't tremble with fear. I am your God. I will make you strong, as I protect you with my arm and give you victories."*

Personalize this with your name: Al. Katherine, Michelle, Shelia ...

> *"Don't be afraid. I am with <<Name>>. Don't tremble with fear. I am <<Name>>'s God. I will make <<Name>> strong, as I protect <<him/her>> with my arm and give <<Name>> victories."*

Deuteronomy 20:1 in the Message Bible says:

> *"... In a few minutes you're going to do battle with your enemies. Don't waver in resolve. Don't fear. Don't hesitate. Don't panic. God, your God, is right there with you, fighting with you against your enemies, fighting to win."*

6. When facing adversity ... tell your circumstances and those around you to "Hush."

Sometimes you don't even have to tell your friends ... more properly known as acquaintances ... to hush ... because at the first sign of adversity ... they're gone faster than a hot chocolate pie at a church picnic.

However, for those who either comment before bolting or hang around ... *never let the second voice distract you from what you know to be spiritual truth and your ability to allow His power to work through you.*

Have you ever thought about how you want others to perceive you ... *what you want them to say and/or think about you?*

Truthfully, I can think of several ways I'd want to be spoken of ... *but none more satisfying* than what's found in Mark 4:41 in the Message Bible which says:

> *"They were in absolute awe, staggered. 'Who is this, anyway?' they asked. 'Wind and sea at his beck and call!'"*

You're probably thinking ... yes, but that was Jesus. I understand ... but I can also quote John 14:12 in the Amplified Bible which says:

> *"I assure you, most solemnly I tell you, if anyone steadfastly believes in Me, he will himself be able to do the things that I do; and he will do even greater things than these, because I go to*

the Father."

7. Always be willing to learn in every situation.

Philippians 4:11 in the New Living Translation says:

> *"I'm not saying this because I'm in any need. I've learned to be content in whatever situation I'm in."*

I've gone through some things in my life ... and I've wanted to learn everything I could in those situations ... so I would never have to experience them again.

Philippians 4:12 in the New Living Translation says:

> *"I know how to live on almost nothing or with everything. I have learned the secret of living in every situation, whether it is with a full stomach or empty, with plenty or little."*

God clearly wants us to learn how to live in every situation, circumstance, problem and/or adversity that we face.

I strongly suggest you meditate on Philippians 4:13 in the Message Bible which says:

> *"Whatever I have, wherever I am, I can make it through anything in the One who makes me who I am."*

The only way He can make you who He wants you to

be ... is by your willingness to learn from every situation you face.

One final scripture in this teaching ... 2 Corinthians 1:3-4 in the Message Bible says:

"All praise to the God and Father of our Master, Jesus the Messiah! Father of all mercy! God of all healing counsel! He comes alongside us when we go through hard times, and before you know it, he brings us alongside someone else who is going through hard times so that we can be there for that person just as God was there for us."

Your Heavenly Father is teaching you His way ... 24 hours a day.

RichThoughts for Breakfast Volume 9

Day 12

10 Things You Need to Know About Deception

There was a time when being deceptive would not be tolerated … but anymore, it seems to be the norm in advertising … permissible in politics … encouraged on some dating sites … tolerated in some workplaces … but none of that makes it right. In fact, it's scripturally wrong.

So today let's talk about deception … where it began, how to recognize and overcome it.

According to dictionary.com deceit means

> **"concealment or distortion of the truth for the purpose of misleading; fraud; cheating:"**

Self-deception is the process or fact of misleading ourselves to accept as true or valid what is false or invalid.

The first case of deception and false advertising began in the Garden of Eden.

Everything was perfect ... perfect place to live ... great food to eat ... perfect husband ... God even told them where all the gold and jewels were ...

But yet deception entered the house ...

We're going to expose the three cunning characteristics of deception found in the Garden.

#1 – Satan wants to create doubt and unbelief in the promises of God.

Genesis 3:1 in the Amplified Bible says:

> *"NOW THE serpent was more subtle and crafty than any living creature of the field which the Lord God had made."*

The Message Bible says he was *clever, more clever than any other.*

Have you ever noticed how clever advertisers are? Unfortunately, I don't have time to go into that today.

#2 – The enemy tries to create confusion over what God has said.

Genesis 3:1 in the Amplified Bible says:

> *"And he [Satan] said to the woman, Can it really be that God has said, You shall not eat from every tree of the garden?"*

Eve must have wondered what God meant when he said you shall not eat of every tree of the garden ... there was only one tree she wasn't to eat from ...

It's a trick of Satan to try and confuse the word of God ...

<u>Confusion and doubt are two of the enemy's greatest weapons.</u>

He'd love to keep us confused and *doubting the promises of God.*

#3 – Satan tries to imply that she is being deprived by God ... that something was missing in her life.

Genesis 3:4 says:

> *"And the serpent said unto the woman, Ye shall not surely die:"*

You're being deprived of this ... think about what television advertising tries to do.

Your life will be so much better if you drive this car, wear that perfume, stay at this resort, wear these diamonds ... **you know what I'm talking about** ...

Do you know when you're being deceived? Would it be deception if you knew it?

Bottom line, don't put yourself in a place where you can be deceived.

What is the set up for deception?

1. Exaggerating or overstating the facts.

Genesis 3:2-4 says:

> "And the woman said unto the serpent, We may eat of the fruit of the trees of the garden: But of the fruit of the tree which is in the midst of the garden, God hath said, Ye shall not eat of it, neither shall ye touch it ..."

God did not say she couldn't touch the fruit ... He said she couldn't eat the fruit.

She overstated the restriction ...

When you overstate something ... *that's like lying* ... putting yourself in the position for trouble.

2. Understating the consequences; not connecting the dots or completing the picture.

Let's look at Genesis 3:2-3 one more time.

> "And the woman said unto the serpent, We may eat of the fruit of the trees of the garden: But of the fruit of the tree which is in the midst of the garden, God hath said, Ye shall not eat of it, neither shall ye touch it, lest ye die."

She said lest you die ... meaning you could die ... but God said you will die.

Somebody is not connecting the dots ...

All wrong decisions have painful consequences ... that's deception ...

If you think you can bypass the rules or that they only apply to everybody else ... that's deception.

Thinking you can spend more than earn ... *without consequences* ... that's deception.

3. The fruit looked good, pleasant, and desirable ... it had all the ingredients for addiction ...

Genesis 3:6 says:

> "And when the woman saw that the tree was good for food, and that it was pleasant to the eyes, and a tree to be desired to make one wise, she took of the fruit thereof, and did eat, and gave also unto her husband with her; and he did eat."

Buying that big screen TV might be good for a season ...

The boat you bought ... fun for a while, till you find out how much it costs to operate it.

The pleasure of sin is good for a season but then you die ... Hebrews 11:25.

<u>Here are two destructive ways to respond to sin</u>

and guilt:

1.   Hide, try to cover up your shame.

Genesis 3:7, 10-11 in the Amplified Bible says:

> *"Then the eyes of them both were opened, and they knew that they were naked; and they sewed fig leaves together and made themselves apron like girdles. He said, I heard the sound of You [walking] in the garden, and I was afraid because I was naked; and I hid myself. And He said, Who told you that you were naked? Have you eaten of the tree of which I commanded you that you should not eat?"*

Have you seen the latest movie? No ... then you should decide on whether it's appropriate before you buy that ticket.

Well ... don't you think I have to experience sin to know that I shouldn't do it? *Shouldn't I see the movie to know if it's okay or not?*

Adam and Eve brought into the world something that wasn't there before ... sin ... don't play their game.

2.   Play the blame game ... it's not my fault.

Genesis 3:12-13 in the Amplified Bible says:

> *"And the man said, The woman whom You gave to be with me--she gave me [fruit] from the tree,*

> and I ate. And the Lord God said to the woman, What is this you have done? And the woman said, The serpent beguiled (cheated, outwitted, and deceived) me, and I ate."

The devil made me do it ... the iconic phrase from comedian Flip Wilson ... if the devil can make you do it, *that means he has authority over you and that is in direct conflict with the Word of God.*

When you blame somebody else, you will never experience true repentance.

But then you do foolish things when you're living in deception.

We've reached what the title of this teaching is about:

10 Things You Need to Know About Deception ...

1. When you're being deceived you don't recognize the deception.

Jeremiah 9:6 in the New International Version says:

> "'You live in the midst of deception; in their deceit they refuse to acknowledge me,' declares the LORD."

2. How do you become deceived?

2 Corinthians 4:4 in the Amplified Bible says:

> "For the god of this world has blinded the unbelievers' minds [that they should not discern the truth], preventing them from seeing the illuminating light of the Gospel of the glory of Christ (the Messiah), Who is the Image and Likeness of God."

3. Jesus even warned about being deceived.

Mark 13:6 says:

> "And Jesus answering them began to say, Take heed lest any man deceive you."

4. Who deceives you?

Genesis 3:13 says:

> "Then the LORD God said to the woman, 'What is this you have done?' The woman said, 'The serpent deceived me, and I ate.'"

5. People who are deceived are not smart.

Proverbs 20:1 says:

> "Wine is a mocker, strong drink is raging: and whosoever is deceived thereby is not wise."

6. What feeds deception?

1 Corinthians 15:33 in the Amplified Bible says:

> "Do not be so deceived and misled! Evil com-

panionships (communion, associations) corrupt and deprave good manners and morals and character."

7. God does not like deception.

Proverbs 8:7 in the New Living Translation says:

> "For I speak the truth and detest every kind of deception."

8. Deception puts you in bad company.

1 Corinthians 6:9 in the Amplified Bible says:

> "Do you not know that the unrighteous and the wrongdoers will not inherit or have any share in the kingdom of God? Do not be deceived (misled): neither the impure and immoral, nor idolaters, nor adulterers, nor those who participate in homosexuality."

9. There is no deception among those who move in Godly authority.

John 7:18 in the Amplified Bible says:

> "He who speaks on his own authority seeks to win honor for himself. [He whose teaching originates with himself seeks his own glory.] But He Who seeks the glory and is eager for the honor of Him Who sent Him, He is true; and there is no

unrighteousness or falsehood or deception in Him."

10. Out of the abundance of your heart something will speak.

Job 15:5 in the New Living Translation says:

"Your sins are telling your mouth what to say. Your words are based on clever deception."

RichThoughts for Breakfast Volume 9

Day 13

God Is Looking for Real Men

The Lord recently directed me to read the entire chapter of Psalm 112. There are ten verses in the chapter and within it, the Lord showed me ten qualities of a real man.

1. A real man will fear the Lord and delight in His Word.

Psalm 112:1 in the Amplified Bible says:

> "PRAISE THE Lord! (Hallelujah!) Blessed (happy, fortunate, to be envied) is the man who fears (reveres and worships) the Lord, who delights greatly in His commandments."

In Job 28:28 in the Amplified Bible the fear of the Lord is linked with wisdom.

> "But to man He said, Behold, the reverential and worshipful fear of the Lord--that is Wisdom; and to depart from evil is understanding."

A real man has an insatiable appetite for the Word of God and He delights in it day and night.

Joshua 1:8 in the Amplified Bible says:

> *"This Book of the Law shall not depart out of your mouth, but you shall meditate on it day and night, that you may observe and do according to all that is written in it. For then you shall make your way prosperous, and then you shall deal wisely and have good success."*

2. The real man can expect his children to make a difference in their generation.

Psalm 112:2 in the Amplified Bible says:

> *"His [spiritual] offspring shall be mighty upon earth; the generation of the upright shall be blessed."*

God wants our children to fulfill their divine destinies … **He wants them to be heroes and not zeroes.**

A real man dedicates himself to see his children raised in the fear and admonition of the Lord, first by his godly example.

Genesis 18:19 says:

> *"For I have known (chosen, acknowledged) him [as My own], so that he may teach and command his children and the sons of his house*

after him to keep the way of the Lord and to do what is just and righteous, so that the Lord may bring Abraham what He has promised him."

A real man will spend time talking with his children about the things in life that have lasting value.

3. A real man will be prosperous.

Psalm 112:3 in the Amplified Bible says:

> "Prosperity and welfare are in his house, and his righteousness endures forever."

A real man not only understands the person of Jesus but he recognizes, practices and adheres to His principles as well.

Whenever we follow His Word, we are embracing the guidelines He sets forth and we will be prosperous.

I particularly like the way my Personalized Promises Bible translates this verse.

> "Wealth and riches shall be in Harold and Bev's house: and their righteousness endureth for ever."

Personalize this verse and make it your own.

4. A real man will always make himself a light in the midst of darkness.

Psalm 112:4 in the Amplified Bible says:

> *"Light arises in the darkness for the upright, gracious, compassionate, and just [who are in right standing with God]."*

I like the Message Bible translation of Psalm 112:4 as well. It says:

> *"Light shines in the darkness for the godly. They are generous, compassionate, and righteous."*

5. A real man is generous and a model of integrity in his business dealings.

Psalm 112:5 in the Amplified Bible says:

> *"It is well with the man who deals generously and lends, who conducts his affairs with justice."*

The Amplified Bible translation of Proverbs 22:29 says:

> *"Do you see a man diligent and skillful in his business? He will stand before kings; he will not stand before obscure men."*

There are so many scriptures about the blessings available to a generous man ... but I feel led to give you Deuteronomy 15:19 in the New Living Translation says:

> *"Give generously to the poor, not grudgingly, for*

> the Lord your God will bless you in everything you do."

I suggest you visit our website, www.debtfreearmy.org and read my blog: "The 12 Benefits of Generosity."

6. A real man is not moved by circumstances and will be remembered for his principles.

Psalm 112:6 in the Amplified Bible says:

> "He will not be moved forever; the [uncompromisingly] righteous (the upright, in right standing with God) shall be in everlasting remembrance."

When a real man faces a challenging circumstance, stressful situation or perplexing problem ... he knows where to turn for his answers.

Numbers 9:8 in the Message Bible says:

> "Moses said, 'Give me some time; I'll find out what God says in your circumstances.'"

7. A real man will not fear any evil or trick of the enemy.

Psalm 112:7 in the Amplified Bible says:

> "He shall not be afraid of evil tidings; his heart is firmly fixed, trusting (leaning on and being confident) in the Lord."

A real man understands that fear is not of God ... it's a lying condition fostered by the devil.

A real man understands the power and peace of mind contained in 2 Timothy 1:7 in the Amplified Bible which says:

> "For God did not give us a spirit of timidity (of cowardice, of craven and cringing and fawning fear), but [He has given us a spirit] of power and of love and of calm and well-balanced mind and discipline and self-control."

8. A real man understands God's purposes will prevail.

Psalm 112:8 in the Amplified Bible says:

> "His heart is established and steady, he will not be afraid while he waits to see his desire established upon his adversaries."

A real man easily overcomes his doubts because he's committed to following God's direction in every area of his life.

Proverbs 19:21 in the Amplified Bible says:

> "Many plans are in a man's mind, but it is the Lord's purpose for him that will stand."

9. A real man is blessed because he knows how to be a blessing.

Psalm 112:9 in the Amplified Bible says:

> "He has distributed freely [he has given to the poor and needy]; his righteousness (uprightness and right standing with God) endures forever; his horn shall be exalted in honor."

There are so many scriptures to choose from that confirm this verse ... but I feel led to share 2 Corinthians 9:8 in the New Living Translation which says:

> "And God will generously provide all you need. Then you will always have everything you need and plenty left over to share with others."

10. A real man's enemies will be destroyed ... not by him ... but by God because of the kind of life he lives.

Psalm 112:10 in the Amplified Bible says:

> "The wicked man will see it and be grieved and angered, he will gnash his teeth and disappear [in despair]; the desire of the wicked shall perish and come to nothing."

With God on your side ... who can be against you?

Romans 8:31 says:

> "What shall we then say to these things? If God be for us, who can be against us?"

Not only will God be on the side of a real man ... but his enemies will be God's enemies.

Exodus 23:22 in the New Living Translation says:

> *"But if you are careful to obey him, following all my instructions, then I will be an enemy to your enemies, and I will oppose those who oppose you."*

These ten things are not meant to be the only ten qualities of a real man ... but they are in fact ... what the Lord directed me to write about today.

Psalm 112 is demonstrating not only the qualities of a real man ... but more importantly ... the characteristics of a godly person.

God is not interested in a man getting in touch with his feminine side ... He wants man to get in touch with Him ... and all the other needs of life will be met.

Fight to Win

Would it surprise you to know that there is a difference between winning and being a winner?

You can win a contest ... the lottery ... an athletic event ... a prize ... but still not be a winner.

<u>Winning is an occurrence ... *something that happens today, this week, this year* and then it's gone</u>. **A winner is someone who recognizes they're fighting for something noble ...** *someone who refuses to quit* **... and who will never give up until they win or accomplish their goal or calling.**

In fact, if you study the history of people who won the lottery ... *you will discover few people who are actually winners in life* ... regardless of the mega-millions they won by having a winning ticket.

Being a winner is a state of mind ... *regardless of what happens or the outcome of any particular contest or endeavor.*

A winner is someone who recognizes they're

fighting for something noble ... *someone who refuses to quit* **... and who will never give up until they win or** *accomplish their goal or calling.*

You and I were created to be winners in the game of life. Yet, *we face an adversary who is dedicated to our defeat* ... however, <u>God instructs us to fight the good fight of faith ... because we're more than conquerors ... who can overcome every attack of the enemy</u>.

As I was pondering this ... I looked up "good fight" and the first reference that I pulled up was 1 Timothy 1:18 in the New International Version of the Bible which says:

> *"Timothy, my son, I give you this instruction in keeping with the prophecies once made about you, so that by following them you may fight the good fight."*

The word *good* is the Greek word *"kalos"* (G2570) which means:

> **"beautiful, handsome, excellent, eminent, choice, surpassing, precious, useful, suitable, commendable, admirable."**

The King James Version of 1 Timothy 1:18 says to us *"... that thou by them mightest war a good warfare."*

The word *warfare* is the Greek word *"strateia"* (G4752)

and it means:

> "an expedition, campaign, military service, warfare."

This particular Greek word *is only used one other time in scripture* ... and that's in 2 Corinthians 10:4 which says:

> *"(For the weapons of our warfare are not carnal, but mighty through God to the pulling down of strong holds;)"*

The Amplified Bible translation of 2 Corinthians 10:4 says:

> *"For the weapons of our warfare are not physical [weapons of flesh and blood], but they are mighty before God for the overthrow and destruction of strongholds."*

I also feel led to share 2 Corinthians 10:3-6 in the Message Bible with you ... which says:

> *"The world is unprincipled. It's dog-eat-dog out there! The world doesn't fight fair. But we don't live or fight our battles that way—never have and never will. The tools of our trade aren't for marketing or manipulation, but they are for demolishing that entire massively corrupt culture. We use our powerful God-tools for smashing warped philosophies, tearing down barriers erected against the truth of God, fitting every*

loose thought and emotion and impulse into the structure of life shaped by Christ. Our tools are ready at hand for clearing the ground of every obstruction and building lives of obedience into maturity."

I want to share a quote with you from Archbishop Nicholas Duncan Williams who said:

"Life is unfair. You don't always get what you deserve. You get what you fight for."

Now let's go back to 1 Timothy 1:18 in the New Living Translation which says:

"Timothy, my son, here are my instructions for you, based on the prophetic words spoken about you earlier. May they help you fight well in the Lord's battles."

The first key to fighting the good fight ... ***of waging effective warfare*** **... of tearing down strongholds is** ***FOLLOWING HIS INSTRUCTIONS.***

Or as I like to say ... READ YOUR BIBLE ... DO WHAT IT SAYS.

<u>*First, we follow the instructions*</u> found in 1Timothy 6:12 in the Amplified Bible which says:

"Fight the good fight of the faith. Take hold of the eternal life to which you were called when you

made your good confession in the presence of many witnesses."

Make your good confession in the presence of many witnesses. Wow ... that could be a teaching in itself.

The second key in fighting the good fight is faith.

I don't feel led to make this teaching about faith. Hopefully, if you listen to our daily Rich Thoughts for Breakfast conference calls or if you have been following our ministry you already know the power of faith.

Let me just say this ...

Faith is not invisible. *Most people think that faith is invisible*, but it isn't. I can show it to you from Scripture.

Hebrews 11:1 says:

> *"Now faith is the substance of things hoped for, the evidence of things not seen."*

Please notice that the thing "hoped for" is invisible, *but faith is the evidence that makes it real*. There is no such thing as invisible evidence.

<u>You can't go into a courtroom and win a case with invisible evidence</u>. *The thing hoped for is invisible. If you have faith for a new house, the new house might be invisible right now but your faith won't be invisible.*

<u>If the faith is invisible, the house will not show up either.</u>

We're fighting the good fight of that which is visible.

How do you make that which is seemingly invisible visible ... you've got to see it in the spirit.

In other words ... <u>see it ... believe it ... confess it ... expect it ... never give up on it ... and manifest it</u>.

One other thing I feel led to share from 1 Timothy 6:12 ... this time from the Amplified Bible translation which says:

> *"Fight the good fight of the faith; lay hold of the eternal life to which you were summoned and [for which] you confessed the good confession [of faith] before many witnesses."*

The verse says ... *"[for which] you confessed the good confession [of faith] before many witnesses."*

The key to winning your good fight of faith is your confession ... *which makes what's invisible ... visible to you.*

If you want to be a winner in life ... *then you must follow the first two keys to fighting the good fight ... following His instructions and having faith.*

The third key in fighting to win ... is to finish what

you've been fighting for.

2 Timothy 4:7 says:

> *"I have fought the good fight, I have finished the race, I have kept the faith."*

My dear friend John Mason in his book *Let Go of Whatever Is Making You Stop* said:

> **"You will be judged by what you finish, not by what you start."**

If you want to finish … you have to have a plan.

No commanding general would ever go into a battle without a plan.

The Dallas Cowboys won their first game of the new National Football League season … *but there had been hours, days, weeks and even months of planning and preparation.*

During the course of a season, the team will face adversities which <u>they must overcome if they want to be victorious</u>.

The team that will lift the Super Bowl trophy at the end of the National Football League season is the one that *followed instructions, kept the faith and finished what they started*.

Child of God, as you fight the good fight … just remember **He makes you a WINNER all the time**.

The late Zig Ziglar, master motivator, said:

> **"You were born to win, but to be a winner, you must plan to win, prepare to win, and expect to win."**

Zig also said:

> **"If you don't see yourself as a winner, then you cannot perform as a winner."**

God's Economic Forecast

Do you want to get really depressed? Would you like to be continually discouraged? Are you yearning for a life filled with financial disappointment?

Then all you have to do ... is listen to television news or read the news on the net or in the papers.

When I think about the media in this country and their forecast, prognostication and assessment of our future, I'm reminded of the chorus that was sung on every *Hee Haw* television show years ago.

> "Gloom, despair, and agony on me, deep dark depression and excessive misery. If it weren't for bad luck, I'd have no luck at all. Gloom, despair, and agony on me."

If you're going through tough times, the **last thing you need is some TV pundit telling you how bad things are** ... *while unwittingly robbing you of all hope.*

Truthfully, Christians should know better than to listen to this drivel.

I'm reminded of another song with a far more positive, upbeat, and yes, scriptural message.

> *"Whose report are you going to believe? We shall believe the report of the Lord."*

"We shall believe the report of the Lord."

Here's an indisputable fact ... if you focus on gloom and doom, then you're going to live with the fear produced by gloom and doom.

But Child of God, in the midst of all the "D" words (depression, despair, disappointment, discouragement, defeat, disaster and debt) ... you need to remember that when you looked out your window this morning, **if you didn't see God's throne fallen from heaven, then He's still on it**.

Throughout American history there have been devastating swings (another "D" word) in our economy oftentimes spreading fear to people willing to listen and fear.

Don't get me wrong ... I'm not saying things aren't tough right now because they are.

The world's system of money is fragile, illusive and can be stolen at a moment's notice. Income may dwindle, stocks plummet and possessions may be lost.

But let me tell you *this attack isn't coming from flesh*

and blood. It's from principalities, powers, rulers of spiritual darkness and wickedness in high places.

John 10:10 in the New King James Version says:

> "The thief does not come except to steal, and to kill, and to destroy. I have come that they may have life, and that they may have it more abundantly."

Unfortunately, way too many people have been unwittingly assisting the thief by unwise purchases and bad decisions. *If you're spending more than you're making, then some of your agony may be self-imposed.*

Make no mistake about it ... the devil will do everything in his power to mess you up. He will show you the "pleasure of living" on a Sakes Fifth Avenue appetite while you only have a Wal-Mart budget.

Financial storm clouds may have darkened your horizon or you may be threatened with a sudden bolt of lightning that came too close. *But you've got to take shelter in His Word and listen ONLY to God's Economic Forecast. For He is the only one who knows what the future holds* and, for sure, He's the only economic forecaster who cares about your having a more abundant life.

God ALWAYS tells His children the truth. He always keeps His Word. He's not moved by what politicians or special interest groups say. He doesn't care about Nielsen TV ratings ... **He just wants what's best for**

you.

When God talks, we'd better be listening and doing what He says.

God has always supplied for His people even when they doubted or did things that weren't so smart. You just have to read the account of the children of Israel traveling through the wilderness to understand the lengths He went to prove His love for His children.

In 1 Kings Chapter 8, we read where, in one day, **God enabled Elijah to defeat and destroy the 450 prophets of Baal, pray rain into a drought-stricken land and outrun King Ahab's chariot for a distance of twenty miles**.

Despite all the blessings and victories, <u>*despite how many times Elijah had seen God move supernaturally in His behalf*</u> ... he took off running because of just one bad report from a crazy queen.

Elijah ended up in a place where there was seemingly no provision and no apparent way to get any. *But God supplied Elijah in a miraculous way by sending ravens, a most unlikely bird, to bring him food.*

When Elijah looked with his natural eyes he couldn't see how provision was possible, *but God opened supernatural ways to take care of his needs. He only required Elijah to remain faithful to the journey he was on* and not get worried or off course.

Our Heavenly Father is no respecter of persons (Acts 10:34). **What He has done for anybody else, He has to do for you.**

God delivered Elijah from people, yes, even those in positions of authority who wanted to take all he had, including His life. It may seem that some of your creditors have those same predatory instincts but, just remember, God is on your side.

One scripture I frequently quote is Romans 8:31 which says:

> "... If God be for (you), who can be against (you)?"

It doesn't matter what's reported on the nightly news; *it doesn't matter what your neighbor or a family member says*; it only matters what the Word of God says.

I could give you dozens, if not hundreds of scriptures, but I'm only going to give you one.

Psalm 84:11 says:

> "For the LORD God is a sun and shield: the LORD will give grace and glory: no good thing will he withhold from them that walk uprightly."

Personalize this scripture with your name ... Lois ... Sam ... Natalie.

> "For the LORD God is a sun and shield: the

> *LORD will give grace and glory: no good thing will he withhold from <<Name>> who walks uprightly."*

God wants you to believe His economic forecast. He doesn't want you looking over your shoulder in fear of economic or financial ruin.

God is not worried about the gloomy financial forecast.

In fact, He delights in showing Himself mighty in your behalf (2 Chronicles 16:9). He will even take care of your enemies:

Jeremiah 15:11 says:

> *"The Lord replied, 'I will take care of you, Jeremiah. Your enemies will ask you to plead on their behalf in times of trouble and distress.'"*

When you seek God's help ... then you can personalize Jeremiah 15:11.

> *"The Lord replied, 'I will take care of you, <<Name>>. Your enemies will ask you to plead on their behalf in times of trouble and distress.'"*

"But Brother Harold, I don't have any enemies." **Oh yes, you do!**

Debt is an enemy ... sickness is an enemy ... depression is an enemy ... sin is an enemy ... lack of income is an enemy ... a rebellious kid is an enemy ... I could go on and on, but here's the bottom line, anything or *anyone that keeps you from fulfilling your divine destiny is an enemy.*

You may be under attack at the moment, but you've got to know that God is going to show Himself mighty on your behalf. There is going to be an all-star performance.

Luke 1:45 says:

> *"And blessed is she that believed: for there shall be a performance of those things which were told her from the Lord."*

Our Heavenly Father delights in demonstrating His miraculous power to provide when all the world's empty promises fail. *His supply is backed by His promises* and it's His delight to take care of those, like Elijah, *who remain steadfast and unmovable.*

What do you believe about your economic future, and more importantly, Whom do you believe?

One last thing ... Job 1:10 in the Amplified Bible says:

> *"Have You not put a hedge about him and his house and all that he has, on every side? You have conferred prosperity and happiness upon him in the work of his hands, and his possessions have increased in the land."*

25 Ways to Know if You're Ready for a Miracle

Day 16

This is a marvelous day … for miracles …

I want you to get a sheet of paper … I'm going to list 25 ways to know if you're ready for a miracle … I want you to write yes by the numbers where you're ready for a miracle.

If there is an area where you don't feel you're ready … write it out … pray about it and find a couple of scriptures to confess over it.

If you need help … let me know and I'll send you scriptures for your confession.

Let's look at 25 ways to know if you're ready for a miracle.

1. If you believe that God is a miracle-working God, then you're ready for a miracle.

Psalm 86:10 in The Living Bible says:

> "For you are great, and do great miracles. You alone are God."

2. **If you know that God is no respecter of persons, then you're ready for a miracle.**

Acts 10:34 says:

> "Then Peter opened his mouth, and said, Of a truth I perceive that God is no respecter of persons."

3. **If you know that whatever you ask in prayer believing that you will receive, then you're ready for a miracle.**

Mark 11:24 says:

> "Therefore I say unto you, What things soever ye desire, when ye pray, believe that ye receive them, and ye shall have them."

4. **If you understand that it is God who has given you the power to get wealth, then you're ready for a miracle.**

Deuteronomy 8:18 says:

> "But thou shalt remember the LORD thy God: for it is he that giveth thee power to get wealth, that he may establish his covenant which he sware

unto thy fathers, as it is this day."

5. If you're not swayed by your circumstances or situations, then you're ready for a miracle.

2 Corinthians 4:18 says:

"While we look not at the things which are seen, but at the things which are not seen: for the things which are seen are temporal; but the things which are not seen are eternal."

6. If you hold fast to the confession of your faith, then you're ready for a miracle.

Romans 4:20-22 in the New Living Translation says:

"Abraham never wavered in believing God's promise. In fact, his faith grew stronger, and in this he brought glory to God. He was fully convinced that God is able to do whatever he promises."

7. If you are ready to stand strong and not be swayed your situation, then get ready for your miracle.

Romans 4:19-20 says:

"And being not weak in faith, he considered not his own body now dead, when he was about an hundred years old, neither yet the deadness of

Sarah's womb: He staggered not at the promise of God through unbelief; but was strong in faith, giving glory to God."

8. **If you exercise your authority over every attack of the enemy, then you're ready for a miracle.**

James 4:7 says:

"Submit yourselves therefore to God. Resist the devil, and he will flee from you."

9. **If you know that your Heavenly Father will never leave you, nor forsake you, then you're ready for a miracle.**

Hebrews 13:5b says:

"... for he hath said, I will never leave thee, nor forsake thee."

10. **If you realize that even if you stumble along the way you won't be down for long because God has a grip on you, then you're ready for a miracle.**

Psalm 37:24 says:

"Though he fall, he shall not be utterly cast down: for the LORD upholdeth him with his hand."

11. **If you understand that no weapon formed against you can prosper, then you're ready for a miracle.**

Isaiah 54:17 says:

> *"No weapon that is formed against thee shall prosper; and every tongue that shall rise against thee in judgment thou shalt condemn. This is the heritage of the servants of the LORD, and their righteousness is of me, saith the LORD."*

12. **If you continue sowing in the midst of a famine, then you're ready for a miracle.**

Genesis 26:12 in the Amplified Bible says:

> *"Then Isaac sowed in that land [in the midst of a famine], and received in the same year an hundredfold: and the LORD blessed him."*

13. **If you start where you are with what you've got, then you're ready for a miracle.**

2 Kings 4:2 says:

> *"And Elisha said unto her, What shall I do for thee? tell me, what hast thou in the house? And she said, Thine handmaid hath not any thing in the house, save a pot of oil."*

14. **If you realize that God will never give up on you then, you're ready for a miracle.**

Romans 8:32 in the Amplified Bible says:

> "He who did not withhold or spare [even] His own Son but gave Him up for us all, will He not also with Him freely and graciously give us all [other] things?"

15. **If you understand that no one who believes in Him will ever be disappointed, then you're ready for a miracle.**

Psalm 18:30 in the Amplified Bible says:

> "As for God, His way is perfect! The word of the Lord is tested and tried; He is a shield to all those who take refuge and put their trust in Him."

16. **If you want to make a difference instead of an excuse, then you're ready for a miracle.**

Isaiah 6:8 says:

> "Also I heard the voice of the Lord, saying, Whom shall I send, and who will go for us? Then said I, Here am I; send me."

17. **If you know that you overcome the enemy by the blood of the Lamb and the word of your testimony, then you're ready for a miracle.**

Revelation 12:11 says:

> "And they overcame him by the blood of the Lamb, and by the word of their testimony; and they loved not their lives unto the death."

18. **If you leave the old sinful life behind so you live in the freedom of God, then you're ready for a miracle.**

2 Corinthians 5:17 says:

> "Therefore if any man be in Christ, he is a new creature: old things are passed away; behold, all things are become new."

19. **If you realize that if God is for you no one can defeat you, then you're ready for a miracle.**

Romans 8:31 in the Amplified Bible says:

> "What then shall we say to [all] this? If God is for us, who [can be] against us? [Who can be our foe, if God is on our side?]"

20. **If you know that you know it's His desire for you to prosper and be in health just as your soul prospers, then you're ready for a miracle.**

3 John 2 says:

> "Beloved, I wish above all things that thou mayest prosper and be in health, even as thy soul prospereth."

21. If you believe that God will meet all your needs and give you plenty left over to share with others, then you're ready for a miracle.

2 Corinthians 9:8 in the New Living Translation says:

> "And God will generously provide all you need. Then you will always have everything you need and plenty left over to share with others."

22. If you immerse yourself in the Word of God, then you're ready for a miracle.

2 Timothy 2:15 says:

> "Study to shew thyself approved unto God, a workman that needeth not to be ashamed, rightly dividing the word of truth."

23. If you trust that God will perform everything He promised you in His Word, then you're ready for a miracle.

Joshua 21:45 says:

> "Every good thing the Lord had promised them [Children of Israel] came true."

24. If you know God loved you enough to give His only Son that you might have life and have it more abundantly, then you're ready for a miracle.

John 10:10 says:

> *"The thief cometh not, but for to steal, and to kill, and to destroy: I am come that they might have life, and that they might have it more abundantly."*

25. If you're living in expectation for manifestation, then you're ready for a miracle.

Proverbs 24:14 says:

> *"So shall the knowledge of wisdom be unto thy soul: when thou hast found it, then there shall be a reward, and thy expectation shall not be cut off."*

RichThoughts for Breakfast Volume 9

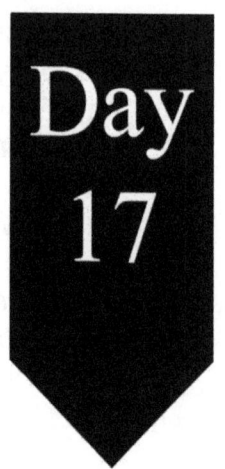

A Hamburger Short of a Happy Meal

Have you ever refused instruction?

If so, *why?*

Was it something you didn't like ... *or perhaps you didn't approve of the person* doing the instructing?

Did you think you already knew everything the instructor would say?

Would the instructions interfere *with something else you already had planned?*

Were you too embarrassed to receive instructions for fear of what others might think?

Did you have an **attitude of indifference**?

Did you think implementing the instructions would not improve *the quality of your life?*

Did you realize the spiritual implications for not receiving instructions?

Proverbs 13:18 in the King James Version says:

> *"Poverty and shame shall be to him that refuseth instruction: but he that regardeth reproof shall be honoured."*

This scripture is one of those ... *"if you do this"* ... *"then this will happen"* verses.

Consider the implications found in The Living Bible translation of Proverbs 13:18 which says:

> *"If you refuse criticism, you will end in poverty and disgrace; if you accept criticism, you are on the road to fame."*

I'd say this scripture is pretty clear ... **if you refuse instruction and/or correction, then you will ... <u>not might or could</u>** ... end in poverty and disgrace.

Let me be direct ... people who are not willing to follow instructions and receive correction are **a hamburger short of a Happy Meal.**

No person in their right mind ... should ever risk the consequences found in Proverbs 13:18:

Consider the words of Proverbs 8:33 in the New Living Translation which says:

> *"Listen to my instruction and be wise. Don't ignore it."*

Here's the bottom line … if you follow the instruction as Proverbs 13:18 in The Living Bible says … then *"… you are on the road to fame."*

Do you want to be <u>*prosperous*</u>?

Do you want to be <u>*successful*</u>?

Do you want to be <u>*happy*</u>?

You're probably thinking that if a person is prosperous and successful then they'll most certainly be happy.

<u>That's not necessarily the case</u>.

First, it depends on your definitions of prosperity and success?

I know people who are very wealthy. In the world's eyes they're prosperous and successful. However, I also know about their home life … *their relationship with their spouse and their children* … truthfully, **they're anything but happy**.

There is a reason that 3 John 2 says:

> *"Beloved, I wish above all things that thou mayest prosper and be in health, even as thy soul prospereth."*

Notice the verse says *"… even as thy soul prospereth."*

There is a direct correlation between your soul prospering ... your growing in the things of God ... **that is linked to your prosperity**, <u>physically and financially</u>.

The Amplified Bible translation of 3 John 2 is even a bit clearer when it says:

> *"Beloved, I pray that you may prosper in every way and [that your body] may keep well, even as [I know] your soul keeps well and prospers."*

The prosperity of your spirit and your soul ... must also be clearly evident to God. This verse says *"... even as [I know] your soul keeps well and prospers."*

The key to prosperity and success is spiritual happiness and that only comes through a personal relationship with the Lord.

Proverbs 16:20 in the New Living Translation says:

> *"Those who listen to instruction will prosper; those who trust the Lord will be joyful."*

Once again, following the instructions ... *leads you to be prosperous and joyful.* The scripture tells us that we should **<u>never ignore knowledge</u>**.

Proverbs 19:27 in the New Living Translation says:

> *"If you stop listening to instruction, my child, you will turn your back on knowledge."*

When we obey His voice … when we <u>follow His teachings</u> … when we *heed the words of His prophets*, **teachers**, pastors, <u>*evangelists and apostles*</u> … then we're headed in the right direction.

Proverbs 13:18 also says: *"… but he that regardeth reproof shall be honoured."*

According to Strong's Concordance the word *reproof* is defined as:

> **"reproof, rebuke, correction, argument."**

Most of the other translations use the word *correction*.

Proverbs 10:17 in the New Living Translation says:

> *"People who accept discipline are on the pathway to life, but those who ignore correction will go astray."*

The scripture is very clear about those who ignore correction.

Proverbs 12:1 in the New Living Translation says:

> *"To learn, you must love discipline; it is stupid to hate correction."*

I like the Message Bible Translation of Proverbs 12:1 which says:

> *"If you love learning, you love the discipline that goes with it— how shortsighted to refuse correction!"*

In other words, **if you love learning** … <u>you'll love discipline, instruction and correction</u>.

Proverbs 15:32 in the New Living Translation says:

> *"If you reject discipline, you only harm yourself; but if you listen to correction, you grow in understanding."*

One other scripture comes to mind. It's Proverbs 23:12 in the Message Bible.

> *"Give yourselves to disciplined instruction; open your ears to tested knowledge."*

It's very important to have <u>an open mind and an open heart</u> … ready to **receive instruction and correction**. We all need to make necessary adjustments as we travel on and continue our journey to the debt free and abundant life that God has ordained for us.

Psalm 119:97 in the Message Bible says:

> *"Oh, how I love all you've revealed; I reverently ponder it all the day long. Your commands give me an edge on my enemies; they never become obsolete. I've even become smarter than my teachers since I've pondered and absorbed your counsel. I've become wiser than the wise old*

sages simply by doing what you tell me. I watch my step, avoiding the ditches and ruts of evil so I can spend all my time keeping your Word. I never make detours from the route you laid out; you gave me such good directions. Your words are so choice, so tasty; I prefer them to the best home cooking. With your instruction, I understand life; that's why I hate false propaganda."

Why does He want us willing to receive His instruction? The answer is found in the New Living Translation of 1 Timothy 1:5 which says:

"The purpose of my instruction is that all believers would be filled with love that comes from a pure heart, a clear conscience, and genuine faith."

We're given a clear scriptural choice when it comes to instruction and correction.

Proverbs 13:18 in the Message Bible says:

"Refuse discipline and end up homeless; embrace correction and live an honored life."

I also want to point out that correction is not judging. The Bible clearly says that we are to *correct, rebuke and be bold to those who are sinning* by not following His instructions.

If we do not offer Godly correction ... we are, perhaps, allowing someone to die in sin.

James 5:20 in the New Living Translation says:

> *"You can be sure that whoever brings the sinner back will save that person from death and bring about the forgiveness of many sins."*

Let me give you another reason why you should desire to tolerate correction.

2 Timothy 3:16-17 says:

> *"All scripture is given by inspiration of God, and is profitable for doctrine, for reproof, for correction, for instruction in righteousness: That the man of God may be perfect, thoroughly furnished unto all good works."*

According to Strong's Concordance ... the Greek word for *profitable* (G3726) means:

> **"advantage, profit."**

The Greek word for *correction* (G1882) means:

> **"correction, improvement of life or character."**

Instruction brings correction which produces profit and advantages in our lives.

As I said earlier, people who flat out ignore instruction and correction ... are a hamburger short of a Happy Meal.

But those who listen to the Spirit and the things the man and woman of God teach will be blessed.

Our precious ministry friend, Miya from Detroit, wrote us.

> I placed the "Payday Is Coming" stickers you sent on a letter from the IRS for my business. They said I owed almost $4K in penalties for filing the return late. There was no tax due just penalty. I believed God that this debt would be destroyed supernaturally.
>
> I stood on my faith and called the customer service agent. "Miss Jo" informed me there was a one-time removal option because I had a history of filing on time. She said the entire penalty would be removed and I'd be receiving a letter indicating the same.
>
> On July 27 I received the letter saying it was removed. One more thing ... when Miss Jo said the penalty was removed, I hollered, "Thank You, Jesus," and Miss Jo quickly said, "Amen." I then said, "And you, too, Miss Jo."
>
> I have enclosed a copy of the letter I received as my proof that God is a debt destroying - faithful loving God - He is my refuge!

What Your Inheritance Should Include

Day 18

Proverbs 19:14 says:

"House and riches are the inheritance of fathers: and a prudent wife is from the LORD."

When I first read this scripture I felt like God might want me to write about the joy of having a "prudent and understanding" wife. Immediately, I *started having warm, fuzzy thoughts about my fine wife, Bev.*

I began to *recall the long list of character qualities and most excellent things about my wife.* I was getting fired up about the prospect of writing about my "smoking hot wife" to use the contemporary vernacular, however, as I continued meditating, the Lord directed me to write about fathers giving their children an inheritance of house and riches.

Oh well, Honey … I'll write about you another day. Now, back to the teaching.

In searching Proverbs 19:14 in the Strong's Concordance I found that *house* means exactly what we'd expect ... *"a dwelling place."*

Inheritance is just that ... something that is passed from one generation to the next.

I've heard those who promote a poverty mentality say that riches are just **"an inner peace, a feeling of comfort and spiritual satisfaction."**

That's absurd *because the Bible proves otherwise*.

In the Strong's Concordance *riches* is the Hebrew word *hown* (hon e) (H1952) and it means:

"**wealth, riches, substance.**"

According to dictionary.com ... wealth, riches and substance are defined as follows:

Wealth: "a great quantity or store of money, valuable possessions, property, or other riches."

Riches: "having wealth or great possessions; abundantly supplied with resources, means, or funds; wealthy."

Substance: "possessions, means, or wealth."

I think anyone who doesn't have a hidden or opposing agenda *would have to admit that the reference to house and riches* in Proverbs 19:14 is definitely talking about money and possessions.

The Hebrew word (hon e) *hown* appears in 26 verses in the King James Version of the Bible.

Psalm 112:3 says:

> "Wealth and riches shall be in his house: and his righteousness endureth for ever."

Personalize it ... Sammie ... Wanda ... Justin ...

> "Wealth and riches shall be in <<Name>>'s house: and <<his/her>> righteousness endureth for ever."

Psalm 119:14 says:

> "I have rejoiced in the way of thy testimonies, as much as in all riches."

I also like the Contemporary English Version of Psalm 119:14:

> "Obeying your instructions brings as much happiness as being rich."

Proverbs 3:9 says:

> "Honour the LORD with thy substance, and with the firstfruits of all thine increase."

Proverbs 6:31 says:

> "But if he be found, he shall restore sevenfold; he shall give all the substance of his house."

Proverbs 24:4 in the Amplified Bible says:

> "And by knowledge shall its chambers [of every area] be filled with all precious and pleasant riches."

I could go on listing the scriptures that have the Hebrew word *hown* in their text. But, I trust that you're getting the picture. **When the Word of God says house and riches ... it is not just a good feeling ... the words mean exactly what the scripture says it means.**

Now let's go a little further.

Proverbs 13:22 says:

> "A good man leaveth an inheritance to his children's children: and the wealth of the sinner is laid up for the just."

According to Strong's Concordance the word *good* is the Hebrew word (tovv e) *towb* (H2896) and it means:

> **"good, pleasant, rich, agreeable, prosperous, understanding, excellent."**

I think it's fair to say that a *good man*, as defined in

the scripture, is also a rich and prosperous man.

Interestingly enough this word (tovv e) *towb* is used seven times in Genesis 1 where the scripture says *"... and God saw that it was good."*

To me, that gives a little more "oomph" to the word *good*. I mean ... we're comparing a good man with the same word ... used to define creation.

The New Living Translation of Proverbs 13:22 says:

> *"Good people leave an inheritance to their grandchildren, but the sinner's wealth passes to the godly."*
>
> *"... but the sinner's wealth passes to Katherine."*
>
> *"... but the sinner's wealth passes to Paul."*
>
> *"... but the sinner's wealth passes to James."*
>
> *"... but the sinner's wealth passes to Terri."*

Personalize it.

So we've established that a good man/woman ... leaves an inheritance to their grandchildren.

Again, there are some who say that inheritance is of a spiritual nature ... *no question that a good man will leave his grandchildren a legacy of spiritual insight ... plus a good name ... the wisdom of his experience ...*

however, that's not what this scripture is saying ... if you look up the word translated from the original Hebrew.

According to Strong's Concordance the word *inheritance* is the Hebrew word (na hael) *nachal* (H5157) and it means:

"to get as a possession, acquire, inherit, possessions and property."

The word (na hael) *nachal* according to the Hebrew Concordance of the King James Bible is in scripture a total of 64 times in 59 verses and 49 of those times it's translated as *inheritance or inherit*.

As I scanned those verses ... it's very clear ... the word (na hael) *nachal is not referring to something intangible* but rather *something totally tangible* as in property and possessions.

It's obvious that one of the qualities of a good man is that he leaves an inheritance of a tangible nature to his grandchildren.

I'm not saying that every person should leave an inheritance the size of the Rockefeller or Buffet estates. It's relative.

But the scripture is clear ... that you are to leave an inheritance ... and if you scan the use of the word (na hael) *nachal, you will notice that it's generally not associated with chump change; broken down cars; or debt-laden stuff.*

<u>Recently I read where it's expected that over $10 trillion dollars will be transferred through inheritances over the next two decades.</u> The average inheritance is estimated to be around $200,000. If that's the average, there will obviously be those who receive much less and those who receive much more.

Here are seven tips that can help protect your hard-earned money and ensure that it gets where you want it to go and not in the coffers of the IRS.

1. Review your current wills and/or living trusts particularly after moving to another state.
2. Consider using a living trust if you don't have one. A living trust will help avoid probate, reduce legal fees, and allow your beneficiaries to pay the least possible in taxes.
3. Be specific about who gets what to avoid family fights. There are certain legal terms you can use to specify heirs ... an attorney will know.
4. Determine whether or not you may need two living trusts depending on the size of your estate.
5. Maximize the benefits of life insurance.
6. Prepare all legal documents including a fully executed Power of Attorney in case a parent becomes incapacitated.
7. Talk with a GOOD CPA and several financial planners ... get multiple opinions.

There is a reason the scriptures discuss inheritance.

Don't put off doing what needs to be done.

Day 19

God Wants Us to Win Every Time

"There's a winner every time" is much more than a carney at a local country fair trying to lure in unsuspecting people to relieve them of their hard-earned cash.

Yes, there is a winner every time … but the real point is … what you win isn't worth having … unless you win a dozen or more times … then you can trade for a decent prize *which you could have actually purchased for 2/3 less than what you spent being a winner.*

This teaching isn't about local county fairs … even though this is the time of the year for such events … but today, I feel led to share how you can be a real WINNER … a scriptural WINNER … a bondage-breaking, yoke destroying WINNER every time.

God wants us to win … EVERY TIME.

2 Corinthians 2:14 says:

> "Now thanks be unto God, which ALWAYS CAUSETH US TO TRIUMPH in Christ …"

The Bible plainly states that Jesus disarmed Satan and all his demon hoards.

Colossians 2:15 in the Amplified Bible says:

> "(God) disarmed the principalities and powers that were ranged against us and made a bold display and public example of them, in triumphing over them in Him and in it (the cross)."

Remember the Word of God says we are always supposed to triumph, *not just 51 percent* of the time, *not even 85 percent* of the time, but always.

How much easier this sounds when we realize Satan has no weapon that will work against us.

Isaiah 54:17 says:

> "No weapon that is formed against thee shall prosper; and every tongue that shall arise against thee in judgment thou shalt condemn ..."

It's important for you to understand that **You Have a Part in the Battle**.

Please notice that this passage doesn't say *God* will condemn the tongues that rise up against you. *It says **you** will condemn them.*

<u>Misinformed teachers have been telling the Body of Christ that God will handle everything for them</u>. ***God is not going to fight our battles for us when He***

has already given us the overcoming power to use on the enemy.

Hear it again. **God always causes *us* to triumph.** <u>God expects us to take the offensive against the enemy and drive him out of his strongholds</u>.

If you are going to have victory, you will have to participate in the battle. **You will have to fight the good fight of faith.** *You will have to put your foot down on the devil's head.*

Remember that your victory over the devil is not supposed to be a once-in-a-while event. **God sees you winning every battle, every time.** He sees you as instant in season and out of season. *The Word clearly says the constant state of victory is your God-given heritage.* It is your birthright.

Romans 8:37 says:

> *"... we are more than conquerors through him that loved us."*

God envisions you speaking forth His Word and treading down every enemy that opposes His will.

Too often I hear misinformed Christians say, *"I just know the Lord is going to take care of my financial problems for me." "The Lord will take care of my backsliding wife." "The Lord will see about my child who is on drugs."*

How full of faith these words sound! However, when the Lord doesn't take care of the situation, when the evil day comes and goes and nothing improves, *these same folks immediately try to patch up their misconceptions* by saying, *"Well, I guess God was trying to teach me a lesson."*

Nonsense! **When we do not pull down the works of the devil, when we just leave it all up to God, then our ignorance gives occasion for the enemy to succeed.** *We are not supposed to be basket cases left in God's care.* We are to be actively involved with God in the business of the Kingdom.

One of the primary works in the Kingdom is to cast down and destroy all the works that the devil has over us. *We are to do what God says to do ... that is how we defeat the enemy.*

Wake up! God is your Father, and He is a good one!

Good fathers don't teach their children by putting him through trials and tribulations.

Good fathers teach obedient children by their words. God is *teaching you by His Word so you can rise up and become the strong warrior* He envisions you to be, *a warrior who will walk in all the authority He has given you.*

Child of God, it is your heritage to be an overcomer.

1 John 5:4 says:

> "For whatsoever is born of God overcometh the world: and this is the victory that overcometh the world, even our faith."

These verses are talking about a sure thing! *God doesn't say you **might** overcome the world. He doesn't say you **may** overcome the world.*

God doesn't even say you will overcome the world most of the time. **He boldly says you if you just believe the Word ... you overcome the world, period.** It's the end of the statement.

God expects you to win every time.

God has given you total power over the devil.

Luke 10:19 says:

> "Behold, I give unto you power to tread on serpents and scorpions, and over all the power of the enemy: and nothing shall by any means hurt you."

I've explained the real meaning of this verse before ... but will continue doing it until it becomes second nature to each of us.

The first word in this verse that is translated *power* is the Greek word *exousia*. It means "delegated power" or better said, "authority."

The second word translated *power* is the Greek word *dunamis*. It means *"ability."* **So notice carefully what God is actually saying.** *"I give you authority over all the ability of the devil."*

Are you getting a hold of all of this? **You have total authority over all the ability of the enemy.** Remember, *"... nothing shall by any means hurt you."* (Luke 10:19)

The Bible literally says nothing shall hurt you. **It also says you have total power (authority) over the devil.** *You never have to lose again.* You can always conquer and always triumph in all things.

The Bible says you are going to rule and reign with Jesus (2 Timothy 2:12; Revelation 5:10). You must begin to take dominion over the moves Satan makes against you.

You know if you cannot do a simple thing like getting rid of an evil thought, you will never be able to rule and reign with Christ.

Only *as you learn* to bring your immediate circumstances under control will you be able to *create the atmosphere you need to stop the devil's violations against you*. You have the power, now you must do it.

God is gathering a people who will walk in their heritage, *a people who will not just talk the Word*, but will also walk the Word.

James 2:17 says:

> "... faith, if it hath not works, is dead, being alone."

According to Strong's Concordance the Greek word for *works* is (er a gon) (G2041) which means:

> **"business, employment, that which any one is occupied; that which one undertakes to do, enterprise, undertaking; any thing accomplished by hand, art, industry, or mind; an act, deed, thing done"**

I think it's clear that works is more than being a greeter at church or visiting the sick ... though both are noble and needed. I may just have to teach on this.

Jesus has purchased a victorious and triumphant life for you. It's available to you today. However, *before you will be able to enjoy it fully, you must put the devil in his place.* Remember, his place is under your feet.

Romans 16:20 says:

> "And the God of peace shall bruise Satan under your feet shortly. The grace of our Lord Jesus Christ be with you. Amen."

Once you realize God always causes you to triumph over Satan, you will quickly be able to re-

claim everything he has stolen from you.

Activate Proverbs 6:31 in your life. The Amplified Bible translation says:

> *"But if he is found out, he must restore seven times [what he stole]; he must give the whole substance of his house [if necessary—to meet his fine]."*

When you finally and fully realize you WIN EVERY TIME ... <u>because of who you are in Christ</u> ... **then you can start claiming your seven-fold return.**

Ways to Keep a Good Thing Going

Psalm 16:8 in the New International Version says:

> *"I have set the LORD always before me. Because he is at my right hand, I will not be shaken."*

Hallelujah!

<u>There are two powerful statements in this verse</u>.

First, *"... the Lord is always before me"* is a powerful affirmation and confirmation for every believer.

- Yes, the Lord is always before me ... as I meditate on Him day and night.

- Yes, the Lord is always before me ... *as I make Him the Lord of my life.*

- Yes, the Lord is always before me ... as I have confidence in knowing that He's preparing the way for me.

- Yes, the Lord is always before me ... *as I know He is protecting me from every attack of the enemy.*

- Yes, the Lord is always before me ... *as I worship Him for His goodness, faithfulness and loving kindness.*

However, the first three words of that verse *reveal the key to the realization of every assurance that I've just listed.*

The words **"I have set"** clearly demonstrate that we're the ones who mobilize the presence of God in every CSP (circumstance, situation and problem) of our lives.

Through our actions or inactions ... we determine our peace of mine, our covering and yes, our own destiny.

In other words, Child of God, you determine God's place in your life. **I'm going to ask you seven questions to determine whether or not you put these things before the Lord.**

- Do you set Him before television?

- Do you set Him before working in the yard?

- Do you set Him before girls or guys night out?

- Do you set Him before your career?

- Do you set Him before your finances?

- Do you set Him before your family?

- What place does God hold in your life?

God has given each of us a free will to decide what we do and don't do in and with our lives. The decision is totally ours … *but when we make the right choice* … the God choice by setting Him first in our lives … *then we're protected, promoted and provided for.*

The Amplified Bible translation of Psalm 16:8 says:

> *"I have set the Lord continually before me; because He is at my right hand, I shall not be moved."*

The Lord is to be set *"continually"* before us. We're not to just set God before us in tough times … good times … when we need Him and when we don't.

According to dictionary.com the word "continually" is an action adverb that means:

> **"habitually; without cessation or intermission."**

The New Living Translation says:

> "I know the Lord is always with me. I will not be shaken, for he is right beside me."

When we put the Lord first ... when we set Him above all other things and people, we have the confidence in knowing the He "is always with me."

Not only is He always with us ... but Hebrews 13:5 says:

> "... I will never leave thee, nor forsake thee."

Now let's go a little further and look at the second key point to Psalm 16:8 which in the New International Version says:

> "... I will not be shaken."

Once again let's look at the Amplified Bible translation of Psalm 16:8 which says:

> "I have set the Lord continually before me; because He is at my right hand, I shall not be moved."

"I shall not be moved."

- No matter what the nightly news is reporting ... I shall not be moved.

- No matter whether I get laid off my job or not … I shall not be moved.

- No matter what's happened to my investment portfolio … I shall not be moved.

- No matter if my car breaks down and I don't have money for the repairs … I shall not be moved.

- No matter what's happening with my children … I shall not be moved.

- No matter what the doctor says … I shall not be moved.

- No matter whether or not I'm being evicted from my apartment … I shall not be moved.

<u>Child of God, are you getting this … *no matter what's going on around you or happening to you* … don't be moved by anything or anyone … *except by the Word of the Lord*</u>.

When you go through the adversities of life … you have the confidence in knowing that if you put Him first … *set Him before you … continually* … that He is at your right hand … right beside you and nothing or no one can keep Him from working in your behalf.

The New International Versions says:

> "... I will not be shaken, for he is right beside me."

As I was mediating on the comfort in knowing that the Lord is always right beside me ... He directed me to Acts 2:25 in the Amplified Bible which says:

> "For David says in regard to Him, I saw the Lord constantly before me, for He is at my right hand that I may not be shaken or overthrown or cast down [from my secure and happy state]."

Did you see where it says, *"I may not be shaken or overthrown or cast down"* ... now get this next part ... *"from my secure and happy state."*

Praise the Lord ... no matter what's going on ... irregardless of your circumstances, situations and problems (CSP) we have the confidence in knowing that we can be in a secure and happy place ... protected from all harm and every attack of the enemy.

The Message Bible translation of Acts 2:25 says:

> "I saw God before me for all time. Nothing can shake me; he's right by my side."

But let's go a little further to read where verse 26 in the Message Bible says:

> *"I'm glad from the inside out, ecstatic; I've pitched my tent in the land of hope."*

As I read and re-read those words ... I felt impressed to write in this teaching several things that are very clear.

First, you decide ... not your spouse ... your Momma or Daddy ... your pastor ... your best friend ... or anybody else ... you must make a constant decision to put God first in your life.

Second, when you make that decision to keep Him continually in your daily life ... *your thought processes ... then you can have the confidence in knowing that He's at your right hand* ... right beside you ... never leaving ... nor forsaking you ... in whatever storm of life you may be facing.

Third, you will no longer be moved ... swayed ... *affected by attacks of the enemy* or anyone else because you have the confidence in knowing that everything is going to be all right.

Finally, I strongly suggest that you embrace the words of Psalm 16:8 in the Message Bible which says:

> *"Day and night I'll stick with God; I've got a good thing going and I'm not letting go."*

Personalize this ... Ilene, Jennifer, Larry, Al, Ray ...

> *"Day and night <<Name>> will stick with God;*

<<He/she's>> *got a good thing going and <<Name>> is not letting go."*

Child of God, you've definitely got a good thing going … don't let go and don't mess it up.

Worthy to Escape

Luke 21:36 refers prophetically to the imminent rapture of the church. The verse says:

> *"Watch ye therefore, and pray always, that ye may be accounted worthy to escape all these things that shall come to pass, and to stand before the Son of man."*

I was taken by the phrase **"worthy to escape."**

I looked up the word *worthy* in the Strong's Concordance and it's the Greek word *kataxioō* (G2661) which means:

> **"to account worthy, to judge worthy."**

Then I noticed that G2661 is from the root word *axioō* (G515) which means:

> **"to think right."**

In other words ... **"to be worthy"** ... *you have to* ... **"think right."**

"But Brother Harold, I thought it was your faith in action that makes you worthy."

The truth is … **if you don't think right (according to the Word of God)** *then how can you act right?*

A thought precedes every action.

The first thing we're told in Luke 21:36 is to **"watch ye therefore." Anything that you watch first creates a thought.**

Next, **after catching a visible image, then it becomes a thought. After that, we're told to pray.**

In our contemporary society it's impossible *not to catch thoughts that are ungodly*.

It's *not a matter of watching the wrong TV shows … you can be subjected to a trashy commercial* while watching a news program or talk show.

It's *not a matter of listening to the wrong music on the radio,* because *you can hear the inappropriate humor of the deejay*.

It's *not a matter of reading the wrong kinds of books … the cover art on good books can trigger wrong thoughts*.

If you are drawing a breath, **you are daily bombarded with images and words that are not for your spiritual edification**.

The good news is that **your loving Heavenly Father gives you a way to escape anything that is not of Him**. It's found in 1 Corinthians 10:13:

> *"There hath no temptation taken you but such as is common to man: but God is faithful, who will not suffer you to be tempted above that ye are able; but will with the temptation also make a way to escape, that ye may be able to bear it."*

As I was reading Luke 21:36 **the Lord directed me to look at the verse from a perspective different than just rapture preparation**. He showed me that *this particular scripture is more than just an "I'll fly away" verse ... it offers a prescription for living in the nasty now and now*.

The bottom line is this ... **it's impossible for any believer ... who's honest about it** ... *to not <u>catch mental images or audio sounds that trigger thoughts which are ungodly</u>*. That's why the scripture says, "Watch ye therefore and pray."

The great author C.S. Lewis once said:

> **"Enemy-occupied territory is what the world is."**

Around 500 BC, the Chinese General Sun Tzu wrote:

> **"If you know the enemy and know yourself, you need not fear the results of a hundred battles."**

You and I have to be wise to every tactic of the enemy. *With that knowledge we can repel every attack.*

My God-loving Momma always taught me that **you can't stop a bird from landing on your head but just don't let it build a nest.**

Do not entertain thoughts that aren't godly. Don't let them build a nest.

Then the Lord led me to Psalm 71:2 which says:

> "Deliver me in thy righteousness, and cause me to escape: incline thine ear unto me, and save me."

The New Living Translation says:

> "Save me and rescue me, for you do what is right. Turn your ear to listen to me, and set me free."

When you pray ... *He will deliver you to righteousness* ... **He will cause you to escape negative ... self-destructive thoughts through the power of prayer**.

As I read Luke 21:36 one other thing occurred to me.

Are you worthy to escape?

Have you asked Jesus to forgive you of your sins

and proclaim Him as the Lord of your life ... if so, that makes you worthy of escape.

Have you put Him first in everything ... if so, that makes you worthy to escape.

Have you tithed even when times were tough ... if so, *that makes you worthy to escape.*

Have you manifested the fruit of the spirit in difficult, even contentious, personal and professional situations ... if so, that makes you worthy of escape.

Have you spent your time on this earth wisely ... maximizing your time ... fulfilling God's purpose in your life ... if so, that makes you worthy of escape.

Have you been the kind of spouse and parent described in the scriptures ... if so, that makes you worthy of escape.

Have you lived the kind of life that will prompt God to look at you on Judgment Day and say, "Well done my good and faithful servant," ... if so, that makes you worthy of escape.

As I was deciding how to close this teaching ... I came across Psalm 18:3 in the New Living Translation which says:

> *"I called on the Lord, who is worthy of praise, and he saved me from my enemies."*

I couldn't help but laugh as the Word reminded me of one of my favorite African proverbs:

> "When there is no enemy within, the enemies on the outside can't hurt you."

If we want to be worthy of escape ... then we need to think like He thinks and believe it or not ... that's what He wants, too.

That's why 1 Corinthians 2:16 contains great news for us. The Amplified Bible says:

> *"For who has known or understood the mind (the counsels and purposes) of the Lord so as to guide and instruct Him and give Him knowledge? But we have the mind of Christ (the Messiah) and do hold the thoughts (feelings and purposes) of His heart."*

As the possessors of the mind of Christ we are to have His thoughts, feelings and purposes.

Yes, **every believer has the mind of Christ ... but whether or not they use it ... is a totally different matter**.

Yes, you have the thoughts, feelings and purposes of Christ ... when you move in obedience to His divine direction.

Romans 12:2 in the New Living Translation says to let God transform us into a new person by changing the way we think.

We have the mind of Christ ... so how do we change the way we think?

Proverbs 20:5 in the Message Bible says:

> *"Knowing what is right is like deep water in the heart; a wise person draws from the well within."*

How do you draw out the wisdom from the well within ... the mind of Christ ... His thoughts, feelings and purposes?

By locating ... reading ... speaking ... confessing the scriptures that speak to the decision you need to make.

Write out the scriptures ... in your smart phone, iPad, tablet, on note cards or *whatever format allows you to refer to them frequently during the day ... and not just during your quiet time.*

When we know the Word of God ... we are better equipped to prove ourselves worthy.

Now ... that's something worthy to think about.

Are You on the Guest List?

Have you ever wanted to attend a party or a social event ... but you weren't invited?

Have you ever gone to a party or social event thinking that you'd been invited ... *only to discover that your name was not on the list?*

Have you ever attended a party only to be asked to leave?

If you've never had the misfortune to experience any of those three circumstances ... have you ever seen similar situations in the lives of friends or at the movies?

Needless to say ... being told that you're not on the guest list would be rather embarrassing ... *a real blow to the ego.* However, there is one guest list that you definitely don't want to be left off of.

Consider the words of Luke 13:23-25 in the Message Bible:

> *"A bystander said, 'Master, will only a few be saved?' He said, 'Whether few or many is none of your business. Put your mind on your life with God. The way to life—to God!—is vigorous and requires your total attention. A lot of you are going to assume that you'll sit down to God's salvation banquet just because you've been hanging around the neighborhood all your lives. Well, one day you're going to be banging on the door, wanting to get in, but you'll find the door locked and the Master saying, "Sorry, you're not on my guest list."'"*

You already know this ... but I must say it anyway ... *this is one guest list where the snub and consequences would be eternal.* **You definitely want to be on God's list for heaven.**

<u>No matter what problem you're facing ... the only answer is to PUT YOUR MIND ON YOUR LIFE WITH GOD</u>.

The verse goes on to say ...

> *"... The way to life—to God!—is vigorous and **requires your total attention** ..."*

The scripture doesn't say that the way to God is to spend *two hours in church on Sunday morning and one hour on Wednesday night*.

The scripture doesn't say that the *only time you read your Bible is when the rumor mill escalates about layoffs at your current place of employment.*

The scripture doesn't say that *the only time you pray is when someone close to you gets really sick.*

The scripture doesn't say that *you get in God's presence only when you have a desperate need.*

No, the scripture says that we're to give Him our total attention.

What does that mean?

Consider Joshua 1:8 which says:

> *"This Book of the Law shall not depart out of your mouth, but you shall meditate on it day and night, that you may observe and do according to all that is written in it. For then you shall make your way prosperous, and then you shall deal wisely and have good success."*

The words "you" and/or "your" are in this verse six times. When you study this verse, you come to understand that <u>YOU will determine your success based on your observance of what your Heavenly Father considers important ... the principles within the Bible</u>. Let's look at the verse again as I personalize it. I encourage you to do the same thing.

> *"This Book of the Law shall not depart out of Harold's mouth, but Harold shall meditate on it day and night, that Harold may observe and do*

according to all that is written in it. For then Harold shall make his way prosperous, and then Harold shall deal wisely and have good success."

When I focus on His directions ... *when I meditate on His word continually* **... when I give Him my total attention, then I will have good success.**

Notice this passage of scripture doesn't say that I will have good success when ...

... I get my undergraduate, Master's or PhD degrees in business or finance.

... I get the right job at the right business at the right salary with all the right benefits.

... I marry the right person ... drive the right car ... live in the right neighborhood.

... I complete Donald Trump's financial success course.

No, **the scripture says that I will have good success when I meditate on the Word day and night ... when I give my total attention to** *putting the Word to work in my life*. Then and only then, will I truly experience the abundant life that God desires for me.

Here's the bottom line ... <u>*if you want to be successful ... then God must be a permanent resident in your life*</u>.

That's how His guest list works. Just hanging around with Him is not going to cut it.

What Luke 13:23 is saying that <u>even though you may have been hanging around church all your life ... you may have talked the talk ... that's not enough</u>. God must be on the throne of your life.

Going to church won't make you a Christian any more than going in McDonald's makes you a Big Mac. *It's relationship.* It's His Word. *It's a renewed mind.* It's a *righteous life. It's forgetting those things behind and pressing toward the mark*, the prize the high calling ... that is in Christ Jesus.

Any time the scriptures mention something in more than one place ... we can know that God is very serious about your understanding the principle.

Consider the words of Matthew 7:22-23 in the Amplified Bible translation:

> *"Many will say to Me on that day, Lord, Lord, have we not prophesied in Your name and driven out demons in Your name and done many mighty works in Your name? And then I will say to them openly (publicly), I never knew you; depart from Me, you who act wickedly [disregarding My commands]."*

The scripture says that you can prophesy, do many miracles and yet your name may not be on the guest list. That is something worth noting.

The key is seeking God ... *giving Him your total attention when it's convenient and when it's not.* <u>Allow Him to direct your path ... allow Him to give you encouragement when it's needed ... allow Him to not only give you success but freedom as well</u>.

In Romans 6:12 in the Message Bible the scripture says:

> *"That means you must not give sin a vote in the way you conduct your lives. Don't give it the time of day. Don't even run little errands that are connected with that old way of life. Throw yourselves wholeheartedly and full-time—remember, you've been raised from the dead!—into God's way of doing things. Sin can't tell you how to live. After all, you're not living under that old tyranny any longer. You're living in the freedom of God."*

You and I have been raised up *"... into God's way of doing things."*

The only way you can know how somebody does something is to *spend time with them, observe what they do and focus on every word they say.*

One final verse that sums up what I've been sharing with you is found in Matthew 7:13 in the Message Bible:

> *"Don't look for shortcuts to God. The market is flooded with surefire, easygoing formulas for a*

successful life that can be practiced in your spare time. Don't fall for that stuff, even though crowds of people do. The way to life—to God!—is vigorous and requires total attention."

Thousands of books have been written about success, fame, fortune and the good life. But **there is only one book and one author that you need to focus on ... that you need to give your total attention to ... and that's our great God, Jehovah**.

If you want to experience the "freedom of God," live debt free, enjoy a prosperous and healthy life ... *then the only place for you to be is in His Word and His presence.*

He wants, deserves and requires your total attention and when you do what His Word says, then Psalm 32:8 (NLT) will be manifested in your life.

> "The Lord says, 'I will guide you along the best pathway for your life. I will advise you and watch over you.'"

Wow ... now that should make you shout Hallelujah, Shandi or jump for joy.

One last thought, if you want to be on His guest list then you'd better give Him your total attention now.

Day 23

Four Rivers Flowing Out of Eden

This is Bev Herring ... my wonderful husband Harold has given me the opportunity to be a guest teacher ... for RichThoughts for Breakfast.

I'm excited to share with you from my heart.

A few days ago, while studying the Garden of Eden and the kind of environment God wants us living in ... my spirit was stirred as I read Genesis 2:10-14 in the Amplified Bible which says:

> "Now a river went out of Eden to water the garden; and from there it divided and became four [river] heads. The first is named Pishon; it is the one flowing around the whole land of Havilah, where there is gold. The gold of that land is of high quality; bdellium (pearl?) and onyx stone are there. The second river is named Gihon; it is the one flowing around the whole land of Cush. The third river is named Hiddekel [the Tigris]; it is the one flowing east of Assyria. And the fourth river is the Euphrates."

It would not be God to put something in the Bible that has no significance even if we don't see it immediately.

I'm convinced there is amazing scriptural significance attached to the name and function of each of these rivers.

Throughout history ... **every civilization revolves around rivers or sources of fresh water** ... If there's no river ... there are no crops, no harvests and no food. There's no water for the people to drink. *If there's not a river, there's no commerce.*

At the same time, in Ephesians 5:26 the Word says *"we are washed by the water of the word."*

I remember the first time Harold and I flew into Cairo, Egypt. It was one of the most memorable sights I'd ever seen. As far as the eye could see there was nothing but white sand and we were high above the earth in a plane ... then in the distance was a large round green spot surrounding either side of the Nile River. As we approached Cairo you could see the city buildings surrounded by a patch of green.

In essence, a river allowed life, health and success. **Water brings a flowing life force ... without which there would be sickness, poverty and death.**

From the river in Eden came four rivers that flowed out of the garden. It's interesting that in Genesis 2:10 they are called "riverheads."

> "Now a river went out of Eden to water the garden; and from there it divided and became four [river] heads."

Each of the four rivers coming out of Eden are more than just a branch of the river ... they are, in fact, river heads.

According to Strong's Concordance, **the river "head" is defined as the "top, summit, beginning" or if you will, the starting point**. These four rivers had their starting point in the garden of God.

Now let's look at each of the four rivers.

Genesis 2:11 says:

> "The first is named Pishon; it is the one flowing around the whole land of Havilah, where there is gold."

According to Strong's Concordance ... *Pishon* is the Hebrew word *piyshown* (H6376) and it means:

"increase."

I really like that ... our God is a God of increase ... *He's not into poverty, lack and debt.* **He is the God of abundance and increase.** You notice the river was not named "lack" or "need" but *increase!*

That tells us something about our God.

2 Corinthians 9:10 in the New Living Translation says:

> "For God is the one who provides seed for the farmer and then bread to eat. In the same way, he will provide and increase your resources and then produce a great harvest of generosity in you."

John 1:16 in the Amplified Bible says:

> "For out of His fullness (abundance) we have all received [all had a share and we were all supplied with] one grace after another and spiritual blessing upon spiritual blessing and even favor upon favor and gift [heaped] upon gift."

When you experience His increase ... you will always have more than enough.

2 Corinthians 9:8 in the New Living Translation says:

> "And God will generously provide all you need. Then you will always have everything you need and plenty left over to share with others."

If God added the last part of Genesis 2:11 ... then there is something significant He wanted us to take note of:

> "... it is the one flowing around the whole land of Havilah, where there is gold."

Not only does verse 11 talk about increase ... we know what the flowing increase was ... it is still considered a type of flowing wealth today. Is it a stretch to say that increase is wealth? Not if this verse is identifying where the gold could be found.

God not only wants you to have increase ... He wants it flowing into wealth in your life.

Just for the record, we're not talking about fool's gold, or something gold-plated to make it look good without having substance ... we're talking about the real stuff. **God isn't into imitating anything.** He doesn't have to because He owns everything.

Read in Genesis 2:12 which says:

> *"The gold of that land is of high quality; bdellium (pearl?) and onyx stone are there."*

The gold is of the highest quality and it's located with precious and priceless gems.

The second river coming out of Eden is *Gihon* which refers to salvation.

Genesis 2:13 says:

> *"The second river is named Gihon; it is the one flowing around the whole land of Cush."*

According to the Strong's Concordance *Gihon* is the

Hebrew word *Giychown* (H1521) and it means:

"bursting forth."

This river symbolizes a "bursting forth" from the bondage of sin ... partaking of living water where you will never thirst again because there is a continual flow.

John 6:35 in the Amplified Bible says:

> *"Jesus replied, I am the Bread of Life. He who comes to Me will never be hungry, and he who believes in and cleaves to and trusts in and relies on Me will never thirst any more (at any time)."*

John 4:14 in the Amplified Bible says:

> *"But whoever takes a drink of the water that I will give him shall never, no never, be thirsty any more. But the water that I will give him shall become a spring of water welling up (flowing, bubbling) [continually] within him unto (into, for) eternal life."*

The third river coming out of Eden is found in Genesis 2:14 where it says:

> *"The third river is named Hiddekel [the Tigris] it is the one flowing east of Assyria."*

According to the Strong's Concordance *Hiddekel* is the Hebrew word *Chiddeqel* (H2313) and it means:

"rapid."

The verse also talks about flowing to the east of Assyria ... which according to Strong's Concordance is the Hebrew word *Ashshuwr* (H804) which means:

"a sense of being successful."

Sadly, there are a lot of people who believe they've missed their best opportunity to be successful. That's simply not the case. When you tap into His living water ... flowing with increase, salvation and now success ... you can experience a rapid turnaround in every situation you're facing.

In order to be successful ... you must organize and have a plan. **Success is a consequence of the decisions we make and the actions we take.**

The fourth river coming out of Eden is found in the last part of Genesis 2:14:

"... And the fourth river is the Euphrates."

According to the Strong's Concordance *Euphrates* is the Hebrew word *Pĕrath* (H6578) which means:

"fruitful; fruitfulness."

When I think about being fruitful ... I feel that's what God wants us to be in every single area of our lives. Make the most of what we have.

Our greatest treasure is not the balance in our checking account or investment portfolio ... but rather how we're using our time. **Wealth will follow good decisions.**

No question ... God wants us redeeming the time.

Ephesians 5:15-16 in the Amplified Bible says:

> *"Look carefully then how you walk! Live purposefully and worthily and accurately, not as the unwise and witless, but as wise (sensible, intelligent people), Making the very most of the time [buying up each opportunity], because the days are evil."*

God's Garden in Eden had four rivers flowing out of it. Today, **we're God's garden. He wants increase, salvation, success and redeemed time (fruitfulness) flowing out of us into a lost and dying world.**

There were four rivers flowing out of Eden ... God wants them flowing out of you.

What Did You Say That Word Was?

A special thanks to my fine wife Bev for her anointed teaching on Day 23. Honey, God's blessing is on everything you do.

I feel led to read seventeen verses to you. Then, I have a challenge for you. Find the one word that is used in all seventeen verses. A scriptural understanding of this word can have a profound impact on your life and your destiny.

Ready ... here we go.

Matthew 9:22

> "But Jesus turned him about, and when he saw her, he said, Daughter, be of good comfort; thy faith hath made thee whole. And the woman was made whole from that hour."

Matthew 14:36

> "And besought him that they might only touch

the hem of his garment: and as many as touched were made perfectly whole."

Matthew 15:28

"Then Jesus answered and said unto her, O woman, great is thy faith: be it unto thee even as thou wilt. And her daughter was made whole from that very hour."

Mark 5:34

"And he said unto her, Daughter, thy faith hath made thee whole; go in peace, and be whole of thy plague."

Mark 6:56

"And whithersoever he entered, into villages, or cities, or country, they laid the sick in the streets, and besought him that they might touch if it were but the border of his garment: and as many as touched him were made whole."

Mark 10:52

"And Jesus said unto him, Go thy way; thy faith hath made thee whole. And immediately he received his sight, and followed Jesus in the way."

Luke 8:48

"And he said unto her, Daughter, be of good

comfort: thy faith hath made thee whole; go in peace."

Luke 8:50

"But when Jesus heard it, he answered him, saying, Fear not: believe only, and she shall be made whole."

We've covered eight of the 17 verses ... **have you figured out what the word is yet?**

Luke 17:19

"And he said unto him, Arise, go thy way: thy faith hath made thee whole."

John 5:4

"For an angel went down at a certain season into the pool, and troubled the water: whosoever then first after the troubling of the water stepped in was made whole of whatsoever disease he had."

John 5:6

"When Jesus saw him lie, and knew that he had been now a long time in that case, he saith unto him, Wilt thou be made whole?"

John 5:9

"And immediately the man was made whole, and

took up his bed, and walked: and on the same day was the sabbath."

John 5:11

"He answered them, He that made me whole, the same said unto me, Take up thy bed, and walk."

John 5:14

"Afterward Jesus findeth him in the temple, and said unto him, Behold, thou art made whole: sin no more, lest a worse thing come unto thee."

John 5:15

"The man departed, and told the Jews that it was Jesus, which had made him whole."

John 7:23

"If a man on the sabbath day receive circumcision, that the law of Moses should not be broken; are ye angry at me, because I have made a man every whit whole on the sabbath day?"

Acts 4:9

"If we this day be examined of the good deed done to the impotent man, by what means he is made whole."

Did you guess the one word that's in all seventeen scriptures that I've just read to you?

The word is **whole** and it's from the Greek word *sozo* (G4982) which means:

> **"to save, keep safe and sound, to rescue from danger or destruction, to make whole."**

According to Strong's Concordance, the Greek word *sozo* is used a total of 118 times in 103 verses in the King James Version of the Bible.

One prominent Bible dictionary defines *sozo* as ...

> *"saved: The word 'save' in the original Greek is sozo and means: 'safe' or, 'in a state of being saved from things which make you unsound' (examples being, destructive ideas and philosophies held, poverty, etc.), 'to do well', 'to keep safe and sound', 'to rescue from danger and adversity', 'to make whole', 'to restore to health', 'to preserve', etc."*

The Amplified Bible in several verses translates the word *sozo* as "growing in maturity or wholeness."

The Word says that we're to ...

1. Give to the widows and orphans ...

2. Win the lost ... feed the hungry ... cloth the na-

ked ... disciple the found while they're still around.

How are we going to do what the Word of God says when our paycheck runs out before the month does?

Here's another question ... something to think about ... *are you whole when you have a job that you can't stand?*

That's not God's best for us.

When you get married ... according to the scripture ... you become one flesh ... *you are whole as a couple in Him.*

If there is continual stress and strain in your marriage, *then your marriage is not whole.*

Nearly 60% of first marriages end in divorce because of money and debt and nearly 80% of all second marriages end in divorce for the same reason.

The enemy will use division/confusion/deception or *any other tool he can to destroy the unity and wholeness of a marriage.*

A marriage will never be whole ... if the couple lies to each other about money.

Over 58% of spouses lie to each other about the exact price of a major purchase. *Does that sound like a mar-*

riage that's whole to you?

Sadly, I'm continually approached by spouses who have lied to their mate about their spending habits and lifestyle of debt.

I remember one case where a woman ran up over $70,000 in credit card debt without her husband knowing about it. In fact, *she didn't even have a job ... the cards were in his and her names ...* she had the statements sent to a different address.

This lady was living in "La La Land" *because she was convinced her husband would never find out the truth.*

I remember another case where a man took out *a second mortgage on their home to cover business losses so his wife wouldn't know the real truth.*

If the marriage is going to be whole ... *you must sit down and discuss the whole truth about your finances.*

Amos 3:3 says:

> *"Can two walk together, except they be agreed?"*

The Amplified Bible translation of Amos 3:3 even suggests that couples pick a specific time for their discussions. It says:

> *"Do two walk together except they make an ap-*

pointment and have agreed?"

Proverbs 11:5 in the New Living Translation says:

> "The godly are directed by honesty; the wicked fall beneath their load of sin."

It's important that couples stop playing the blame game. **Laying the blame for financial mistakes on each other solves nothing.** Don't fix the blame ... fix the problem.

Proverbs 12:15 in the New Living Translation says:

> "Fools think their own way is right, but the wise listen to others."

Matthew 18:19 in the Amplified Bible says:

> "Again I tell you, if two of you on earth agree (harmonize together, make a symphony together) about whatever [anything and everything] they may ask, it will come to pass and be done for them by My Father in heaven."

<u>I strongly encourage you to write a confession that you both can say about your finances and your marriage.</u> It's important that your confession is the same whether you read it together or separately.

You can move toward wholeness in your marriage and in your life with His help and direction.

Here's one last scriptural reference to meditate on.

Vine's Bible Dictionary says that *sozo* is **"inclusively for all the benefits bestowed by God on man in Christ."**

You've got benefits.

Isaiah 54:17 says:

> *"No weapon that is formed against thee shall prosper; and every tongue that shall rise against thee in judgment thou shalt condemn. This is the heritage of the servants of the LORD, and their righteousness is of me, saith the LORD."*

Your benefits are amazing ... you have a heritage as a servant of the Lord ... He wants you made whole in every area of your life.

Ignorant … Stupid … or Just Naïve

Have you ever heard something that sounded good … even kinda scriptural … but it was wrong?

I once had a man say to me:

> "God is going to provide for me … I don't have to worry. God feeds the birds and he'll feed me and my family too."

Truthfully, I'm not sure if this man was scripturally ignorant, stupid or just naïve.

- **Scripturally ignorant means he doesn't know the truth.**

- **Scripturally stupid means he knows the truth but chooses to ignore it.**

- **Scripturally naïve means he thinks everything will turn out even though he does nothing.**

Whatever way, he took several truths, *connected*

them together to the point that his thoughts were just plain wrong.

First, God does want to provide for you.

Philippians 4:19 says:

> "But my God shall supply all your need according to his riches in glory by Christ Jesus."

Second, God tells us not to worry.

Philippians 4:6 in the New Living Translation says:

> "Be anxious for nothing, but in everything by prayer and supplication, with thanksgiving, let your requests be made known to God; 7 and the peace of God, which surpasses all understanding, will guard your hearts and minds through Christ Jesus."

Deuteronomy 31:6 in the Message Bible says:

> "God is striding ahead of you. He's right there with you. He won't let you down; he won't leave you. Don't be intimidated. Don't worry."

I could list multiple scriptures that would reinforce the ones that I've just given you that prove God doesn't want you to worry and that He will provide for you. Both of these thoughts are true … but the inference that you should do nothing is dangerous.

When it comes to God feeding the birds ... let's look at Matthew 6:26 which says:

> *"Behold the fowls of the air: for they sow not, neither do they reap, nor gather into barns; yet your heavenly Father feedeth them. Are ye not much better than they?"*

If you were to *interpret this verse to mean that you don't have to do anything ... then you would be in error ... serious error.* Not only that, but you would be destined to live a life of mediocrity and insufficiency.

People who adopt this philosophy of life are *as lost a goose in a blizzard when it comes to their finances.* They don't know how to balance their checkbook and I'd venture to say *they don't have a clue what their bank account balance is.*

Similarly, these folks don't have a budget, a spending or a financial plan ... and could *easily develop a victim complex believing nothing is ever their fault.*

The basis for their faulty assumptions is the notion that God will provide for those who do nothing and that's just wrong on so many levels.

Let's be clear ... **Jesus is not telling you that you can become a couch potato *waiting for someone to bring you supper*.**

As I'm typing this teaching ... I'm looking out at several trees with various birds sitting there eyeing their breakfast.

Never once have I seen a worm jump up out of the ground and into the bird's mouth or bird seed fly off the ground into their mouths.

I realize this may come as a shock to some but the *birds have to work for their food. They have to get out of the trees, off the fences and walk through the lawns looking for something to snack on.*

The truth of the matter is, *birds are generally flying at first light ... searching for food. They eat twice their weight because it takes a lot of energy to fly.* Bottom line ... if they didn't work for their food ... they wouldn't eat ... and they would eventually die.

When we work ... when we show ourselves faithful ... God provides for us.

If you don't know how much money you have ... where it's going ... how much debt you have ... a plan to pay if off rapidly ... then you're not a good steward.

Let me ask you a question ... who is least likely to live in anxiety?

The person who knows exactly how much he has ... what he owes and when he'll be debt free ...

Or ...

The person who spends everything they get with

the illusion that they will always be provided for.

The answer is obvious.

Let me also be clear on one other point. There is a difference ... a big difference *between faith and presumption.*

Faith requires trust ... *presumption is an assumption not based on scriptural laws but the lusts of our flesh.*

Years ago, I read a great book by Dr. Fred Price entitled *Faith, Foolishness and Presumption.*

It would be foolish to build the largest, most decadent looking hot fudge sundae you've ever seen ... extend your hand toward it and say, "Calories come out in Jesus' name." *That's not faith ... it's foolishness.*

It's not faith but *presumption to spend more than we earn and think that God is going to supply our needs* ... when we've been foolish.

The birds work very hard to build a nest. *They make hundreds of trips bringing only a beak full of material each time, yet they provide a home for their family.* If a storm of life destroys their nest ... they start all over again.

Yes, God does provide for the birds ... *but He expects them to do their part ... and they do.*

Just as an aside, have you noticed that birds sing

while they work ... they're happy in what they're doing ... *they appreciate the opportunity of living ... and providing for their family is one part of it ...* they are *not moved by circumstances ...* they just keep on ... keeping on.

And by the way, if they have to rebuild their nest ... they're still singing.

Truthfully, certain birds absolutely amaze me ... for instance, the tiny hummingbird. In order to *hover at a flower or feeder*, the hummingbird's wings beat at the rate of 75 beats per second. Now that's what I call work.

During the years that I've been on planet earth I've heard people refer to other people as a "bird brains."

This insult generally refers to the size of a bird's brain ... *and is generally leveled at someone who doesn't think* or *speaks without thinking.*

Here's what I know ... birds have a great work ethic ... they provide for their families and see a world filled with possibilities ... and they're always singing.

Think about this question ... when you hear birds singing, does it make you feel better? For most people, the answer is yes.

Perhaps birds understand Ephesians 4:23 in The Living Bible a little better than most humans. It says:

> *"Now your attitudes and thoughts must all be constantly changing for the better."*

The man I mentioned at the beginning of this call was right in one respect ... we're to never worry ... worry, anxiety and depression are all the devil's anointing.

Philippians 4:6 in The Living Bible says:

> *"Don't worry about anything; instead, pray about everything; tell God your needs, and don't forget to thank him for his answers."*

When we commune with our Heavenly Father ... He always ... *always provides for and empowers us to achievements beyond our natural mind and/or abilities.*

Philippians 4:13 in The Living Bible says:

> *"For I can do everything God asks me to with the help of Christ who gives me the strength and power."*

Make no mistake about it ... God wants us maximizing our stewardship of the things He entrusts to us. *If you want more blessings than ever ... show yourself faithful with what you've got.*

Now that's what I call a bird's eye view of the truth.

Harold Herring

Day 26

Can I Get a Witness in the House?

Have you ever watched a courtroom drama *on television or at the movies?*

Typically, when a witness is sworn in ... they place their right hand on a Bible and are asked if *the testimony they're about to give is the truth, the whole truth and nothing but the truth* ... so help them God.

You may have wondered why they use a phrase ... the truth, the whole truth and nothing but the truth ... *that seems a bit redundant*, doesn't it?

A testimony can either be truthful or it can be false. In the courts of this world ... *if you give false testimony then you perjure yourself* and you could easily end up in jail.

In fact, *the scripture even admonishes us* to never give false testimony.

Exodus 23:1 in the Message Bible says:

> "Don't pass on malicious gossip. Don't link up

with a wicked person and give corrupt testimony. Don't go along with the crowd in doing evil and don't fudge your testimony in a case just to please the crowd. And just because someone is poor, don't show favoritism in a dispute."

Like the natural courts ... our Heavenly Father wants us testifying about the truth, the whole truth and nothing but the truth. That should be easier for all of us ... because He is the truth.

John 14:6 says:

> "Jesus saith unto him, I am the way, the truth, and the life: no man cometh unto the Father, but by me."

Our loving Heavenly Father not only wants us telling the truth ... *He wants us telling the truth about Him ...* His grace, goodness, mercy, forgiveness, love and manifest blessings.

1 Chronicles 16:8 says:

> "Give thanks unto the LORD, call upon his name, make known his deeds among the people."

The Message Bible translation of 1 Chronicles 16:8-9 says:

> "Thank God! Call out his Name! Tell the whole world who he is and what he's done! Sing to

him! Play songs for him! Broadcast all his wonders!"

- When our favorite *athlete does something remarkable* ... we want to talk with all our friends about his/her accomplishments.

- When our *favorite team wins the big game* ... we want to brag on them.

- When we see our *favorite actor/actress give an Oscar worthy* performance ... we want to talk about it.

- When we're *recognized on our jobs* ... we want to tell all our friends about it.

- When we're selected for special *recognition at church or in any sort of activity* ... we want to let people know about it.

- When our children *excel in a sporting event, academic or extra-curricular pursuit* ... we like bragging on them.

- Why, we even *brag on our pets* for doing a particularly good trick, our *cars for their gas mileage or looks* ... *our big screen TVs* ... the list could go on.

There is nothing wrong about the various scenarios I've just listed ... unless *we testify about everybody or everything else except our great God Jehovah.*

The question each of us need to answer is … **how much time do we spend bragging on our God** … *the one who woke us up this morning* … clothed us with the mind of Christ … gave us air to breathe and food to eat?

The scripture is very clear … we're to tell the world "who He is and what He's done."

In fact, the Message Bible translation of 1 Chronicles 16:9 says that we're to *"broadcast all His wonders."*

When the statisticians claim *which "religion"* is the fastest growing … shouldn't it be Christianity? It would be if we are all doing our job.

Colossians 3:15 in the Message Bible is powerful when it says:

> *"Let the peace of Christ keep you in tune with each other, in step with each other. None of this going off and doing your own thing. And cultivate thankfulness. Let the Word of Christ—the Message—have the run of the house. Give it plenty of room in your lives. Instruct and direct one another using good common sense. And sing, sing your hearts out to God! Let every detail in your lives—words, actions, whatever—be done in the name of the Master, Jesus, thanking God the Father every step of the way."*

Can I get a witness in the house?

Let the Word of Christ—the Message—have the run of the house.

Hallelujah!!

"Let every detail in your lives—words, actions, whatever—be done in the name of the Master, Jesus, thanking God the Father every step of the way."

Child of God, our Heavenly Father wants us praising Him and, truthfully, *if we were smart. . .*we'd want to do it a lot more than we do.

Revelation 12:11 says:

"And they overcame him by the blood of the Lamb, and by the word of their testimony; and they loved not their lives unto the death."

The New Living Translation says we "defeat him" by the blood of the Lamb and the Word of our testimony.

You and I have the greatest devil repellant ever devised ... *the thing that ensures his defeat and sends him packing. But if we don't use it ... then it won't work.*

The Word of God encourages us to give our testimony for a very specific purpose.

Matthew 24:14 in the Amplified Bible says:

> "And this good news of the kingdom (the Gospel) will be preached throughout the whole world as a testimony to all the nations, and then will come the end."

God wants us broadcasting the Good News to the entire world. And just for the record, **you don't ever have to leave your hometown to testify of His goodness to the nations.** This is particularly true in certain nations of the world … the United States and Great Britain being perfect examples.

We now live in a global community and *you can testify of God's love to your neighbors and co-workers who've come here from the nations of the world.*

If you do social networking … Facebook, Twitter, Instagram or Pinterest … the world is your forum to tell of His excellent greatness.

You and I have unlimited opportunities to testify of His love to millions of people without ever leaving our homes or offices.

The power of modern technology has brought the fulfillment of 1 Chronicles 16:8 directly into your home.

This is your time to testify.

Luke 21:13 in the Amplified Bible says:

> *"This will be a time (an opportunity) for you to bear testimony."*

When we testify in obedience to His word … *not only are we empowered through our personal devil repellant* … but God makes a promise to all who give testimony to His majesty, love, grace and power.

Psalm 132:12 in the Amplified Bible says:

> *"If your children will keep My covenant and My testimony that I shall teach them, their children also shall sit upon your throne forever."*

When we keep His covenant … *when we testify* … then we ensure that our children will be lifted up … *to sit in a position of honor now and for all eternity.*

Can I get a witness in the house?

Truthfully, that's one of my favorite expressions. I don't have a clue who said it first … but there is so much spiritual truth in it … so I'm going to ask that question once again.

Can I get a witness in the house?

RichThoughts for Breakfast Volume 9

Day 27

The Truth About Mammon

Matthew 6:24 says:

> "No man can serve two masters: for either he will hate the one, and love the other; or else he will hold to the one, and despise the other. Ye cannot serve God and mammon."

I feel impressed to talk about **mammon … a word which only appears in four verses of the King James version of the Bible** … yet it's often misunderstood and misquoted by well-meaning folks.

For most of my life, I heard <u>mammon used as an excuse for being poor and broke</u>. The common thought was:

> "Money is evil because you can't serve God and mammon."

> "God warned us about money because He said you can't serve Him and mammon."

I've discovered that the folks who incorrectly interpret

this verse ... don't really understand what the word means.

So let's begin with the basics.

In Strong's Concordance the word *mammon* (G3126) is the Greek word (ma mo nas) *mamōnas* and it means:

> **"riches (where it is personified and is opposed to God)."**

<u>This verse is actually saying that mammon is when money is a rival to God ... it opposes His desires and plans for His children</u>.

What kinds of riches are opposed to God?

Simply said, *any riches that are used to prevent the children of God from fulfilling His plan and divine destiny for giving them a rich and satisfying life.*

Would it be fair to say that the interest you're paying on your debt ... would be riches that are opposed to God ... because it's preventing you from walking in financial freedom?

Here's a bit of enlightening history for you. <u>The Syrians served a god called Mammon</u>. Additionally, **the Syrians were the first people to create a system of loaning money**. Do you want to guess what it was called? Would you believe *mammon*?

When you're up to your eyeballs in debt ... paying interest ... continually worried because your money runs out before the month does ... then your "riches" are being used in a way that is opposed to God's purposes.

The Mammon god says ... **you can afford the monthly payment** ... but isn't that opposed to God's purpose?

The Mammon god says ... **you can buy now, pay later** ... but isn't that opposed to God's purpose?

The Mammon god says ... **you deserve to buy yourself something special ... you've worked hard** ... *you deserve a break today (and not at McDonalds).*

The Mammon god is selfish ... but our God is generous.

<u>The Mammon god says that if you have the right credit cards, cars, home and jobs, you will be accepted by the right people</u> ... **but mammon lies ... deceives ... entraps ... and destroys**.

If you're buying things with money you don't have, then you trust the world's system instead of the *Word* system.

If you're paying interest on those things you've bought, then <u>you're putting your trust, confidence and faith in the credit card company or lender</u> and not waiting or believing God will provide.

Are you serving God ... *or are you serving the lenders ...* paying them interest ... following their plans for your life?

Who are you serving? Are you serving God or *debt, the god of this world?*

And the real question is ... *does the system of mammon steal your freedom to do the things that God has called you to do?*

The mammon system lures you into debt. Make no mistake about it ... **debt is spending money you haven't earned**.

It's when you're working to satisfy MasterCard's minimum payments ... that your money is not your own ... neither is it available to God's Kingdom ... but rather, it's serving mammon.

Make no mistake about it ... when you're in debt to the *mammon* system, you have indeed become **a slave to an institution that hopes you never quit paying**.

2 Timothy 2:4 in the Amplified Bible says:

> *"No soldier when in service gets entangled in the enterprises of [civilian] life; his aim is to satisfy and please the one who enlisted him."*

Here's the question you need to ask yourself: **"How free are you to serve God and establish His cove-**

nant in the earth?"

I want to ask you that question again, **How free are you to serve God?**

When you're working two jobs just to keep the collection agency from your door, you're not available to God.

The New Living Translation of 2 Timothy 2:4 says:

> "Soldiers don't get tied up in the affairs of civilian life, for then they cannot please the officer who enlisted them."

The King James Version says:

> "No man that warreth entangleth himself with the affairs of this life; that he may please him who hath chosen him to be a soldier."

The Hebrew word for *borrow* means **"entangle, intertwine."**

When we entangle ourselves with creditors (or the mammon system) to the point that we've lost our freedom to do what God has called us to do, then we're not free.

We have so much **stuff** we need to **take care of**, *pay for*, **insure**, *organize*, **fix**, *worry about*, and **keep track of**, *we've lost sight of what God saved us for*. It wasn't just so we could go to heaven when we die.

If your pastor asks you to go on a mission trip but you tell him you can't afford to miss a week of work ... then you're not really free.

If one of your children wants you to be the chaperone on a school field trip *but you can't because you need the income from your second job to help make the car payment* ... then you're not free.

If you're sitting in a church service, a Debt Free Army seminar or another ministry meeting and God stirs you to give an offering of $1,000 ... *but you can't because of the mortgage payment, the home equity payment, the credit card bills* ... then you're not free. You're into the mammon system.

Frederick Saunders, a recipient of the Victoria Cross, which is the highest and most prestigious award for gallantry in the face of the enemy that can be awarded to a citizen of the British Commonwealth, once said:

> **"Mammon is the largest slave-holder in the world."**

Proverbs 22:7 in the Contemporary English Version of the Bible says:

> *"The poor are ruled by the rich, and those who borrow are slaves of moneylenders."*

Moneylenders and the system of mammon are one and the same.

Here's the bottom line ... *if you're up to your eyeballs in debt ... then you're not free to give when God says "Give" or go when God says "Go"* ... you're a servant of the mammon system.

When you're not free to do what God says when He says it ... *you're serving the wrong master ...* **that's unscriptural and contrary to the plan of God.**

The enemy knows this and that's why he lures unsuspecting believers into the bondage of debt. **He wants you serving the lender ... paying high interest rates ... creating mammon that's opposed to the plans and purposes of our Heavenly Father.**

Riches are neither good nor bad ... it's what you do with them that determines their character. **The riches passing through your hands reflects who you are.**

The American writer, Logan Pearsall Smith, said:

> **"Those who set out to serve both God and mammon soon discover that there is no God."**

You've got a choice to make ... do you want to be free? **You can't serve God and mammon ... you can't have it both ways.**

Serve God ... Obey God ... then you will live long and prosper.

Harold Herring

No Second Guessing About Good Living

Philippians 2:14-16 in the Message Bible says:

> *"Do everything readily and cheerfully—no bickering, no second-guessing allowed! Go out into the world uncorrupted, a breath of fresh air in this squalid and polluted society. Provide people with a glimpse of good living and of the living God."*

It's time for an honest self-examination.

Do you and I do everything readily and cheerfully ... *even when we don't want to?*

I will confess to you there are certain things that are part of daily life ... *that I don't enjoy and prefer never to do* ... but sometimes ... I must do them nevertheless.

One of the things that falls into this category is fixing stuff around the house. Before I married my fine wife Bev I told her that I would take her places she'd never been, do things she'd never thought of, but if something broke down at the house ... somebody else was going to fix it.

I've pretty much kept my word ... *but there are moments when it's not prudent, necessary or financially wise to pay someone else to perform a task.*

On those occasions I rise to the challenge ... and as I said, *not always readily and cheerfully* but I'm working on that part of it.

Here's what I've discovered. When I do these "frustrating chores" ... it puts a smile on my fine wife's face ... which I'm sure makes God smile ... *so that's pretty much reward enough right there.*

I smile also ... so not having a desire to fix stuff or be handy around the house ... is not because I can't do it or learn how to do it ... it's just that ... *well*, I don't want to do it.

It's not that I'm lazy ... because I'm not. In fact, I've had several of my mentors over the years tell me I'm the hardest working person they have ever met.

It's just I prefer working hard on things that interest me ... or things I think will further advance the Kingdom ... and the things God has called me to do.

The scripture also says there should be no bickering or second-guessing allowed. If you're drawing a breath and are married ... you've messed up at one time or another.

Even in the best of marriages ... that's going to happen ... unless Walter Mitty (a henpecked husband) marries a Stepford Wife (a wife without an opinion of her own).

I've found that bickering and second guessing among spouses most often occurs over finances.

- "If you'd gotten that raise last year, we wouldn't be in this mess now."

- "If you stayed away from the mall and didn't charge so much on our credit cards we wouldn't be behind on our payments."

Blaming one another ... bickering ... second guessing *never has* and *never will solve a problem* ... and definitely makes things worse ... *so right now*, if this applies to you ... STOP IT. **Practice blame-free conversation.**

As I was searching the scriptures for this teaching ... I came across Job 42:1-6 in the Message Bible which I feel led to share. It says:

> "Job answered God: 'I'm convinced: You can do anything and everything. Nothing and no one can upset your plans. You asked, "Who is this muddying the water, ignorantly confusing the issue, second-guessing my purposes?" I admit it. I was the one. I babbled on about things far be-

yond me, made small talk about wonders way over my head. You told me, "Listen, and let me do the talking. Let me ask the questions. You give the answers." I admit I once lived by rumors of you; now I have it all firsthand—from my own eyes and ears! I'm sorry—forgive me. I'll never do that again, I promise! I'll never again live on crusts of hearsay, crumbs of rumor.'"

Here are Seven things to think about ... whether or not you should be second guessing yourself.

- First, did you seek God before making the decision in the first place? If He directs your steps then forget the second guessing.

- Second, did anything in your decision contradict the Word of God?

- Third, make a list of the reasons you considered in favor of and against making the decision before you did.

- Fourth, now ask yourself ... has anything changed since you made the decision? If not, there's no reason to second guess.

- Fifth, put yourself in a stress-free environment to consider your decision. Maybe going for a walk ... listening to some praise and worship music that lights your fire or doing whatever puts you in a contemplative mood.

- Sixth, this will seem a little strange ... but wash your hands ... I read sometime back that this simple act has the symbolic effect of you washing your hands of the matter.

- Seventh, if second-guessing breaks your focus ... off what God's directed you to do ... then you know where it's coming from.

Let's look at Philippians 2:14 again ... this time in the Amplified Bible which says:

"Do all things without grumbling and faultfinding and complaining [against God] and questioning and doubting [among yourselves]."

The scripture in Philippians also says that God wants us to *"provide people with a glimpse of good living and of the living God."*

Now I got excited about this verse and you should too.

First, it's much more difficult to give people a glimpse of something you're not experiencing or manifesting in your life. So it's time to make the necessary changes to get control of your life and your destiny because God wants to show you off.

- Good living ... is not wondering where your next dollar is coming from.

- Good living ... is not having to work two jobs just to make ends meet.

- Good living ... is not being evicted from your apartment or left homeless through a foreclosure.

- Good living ... is not having credit cards maxed out.

- Good living ... is not worrying about loved ones who're not serving the Lord.

- Good living ... is not spending more on Prozac or worry-related trips to the doctors than you're tithing or giving to the church.

Child of God, the Bible says that your Heavenly Father wants to give other people a glimpse of the good life you're living. If that kind of life is just a dream and not currently a reality ... then you need to begin making the changes necessary to fulfill this direct instruction from the Lord.

Isaiah 3:10-11 in the Message translation says:

> "Reassure the righteous that their good living will pay off ..."

There are three verses in Proverbs that clearly demonstrate God wants you living the good life.

Proverbs 4:4 in the Easy to Read Version says:

> "My father taught me this: 'Pay attention to what I say. Obey my commands and you will have a

good life.'"

Proverbs 7:2 in the Easy to Read Version says:

"Consider my teaching as precious as your own eyes. Obey my commands, and you will have a good life."

Proverbs 19:23 in the Easy to Read Version says:

"Respect the Lord and you will have a good life, one that is satisfying and free from trouble."

I need to move on ... but I'm being led to do a new teaching on how to experience the good life.

When Joshua needed help ... He sought the Lord ... got in His presence ... listened to what God spoke ... and then did what he was told ... so that God's Word could make him prosperous and fill him with success.

Joshua 1:8 says:

*"This book of the law shall not depart out of **thy** mouth; but **thou** shalt meditate therein day and night, that **thou** mayest observe to do according to all that is written therein: for then **thou** shalt make **thy** way prosperous, and then **thou** shalt have good success."*

As you read, confess and possess Joshua 1:8 as your own ... then you will grow into living your life in such a manner that people will get a glimpse of good living through your life. But more importantly, through your manifestation of good living ... **other people will witness the life, promises and power of the living God**.

You will become His success story. Is that possible? Absolutely, if you believe the Word of God ... and I know you do.

RichThoughts for Breakfast

Volume 9

Invite Harold Herring to speak at your church, event, or rally.

Would you like to invite Harold to be a guest speaker at your church, event, or rally? Just send an email to:

booking@haroldherring.com

or call 1-800-583-2963

With a mix of humor, practical strategies, and Biblical insight Harold will inspire, encourage, and prepare you to change your financial destiny and set you on the path to not only set you free from debt but keep you free of debt and living the debt free life God has called you to.

Keep Thinking Rich Thoughts,

Harold Herring

RichThoughts for Breakfast

Jump Start Your Day!!

This motivating start to your day is something no one should be without. I guarantee you will be glad you called in.

Harold Herring

712-432-0900

Access Code 832936#

Playback Daily Call

712-432-0990

Access Code 832936#

The call starts at 8:30 AM EST seven days a week.

Practical Strategies, Biblical Insights and Thought-Provoking Humor

These are just a few of the things you are missing if you're not joining us every day for the **RichThoughts for Breakfast** morning call.

Get Ready to be Inspired, Encouraged, and Entertained.

Your Rich Thoughts are your leap to your future success!

www.ingramcontent.com/pod-product-compliance
Lightning Source LLC
Chambersburg PA
CBHW061255110426
42742CB00012BA/1922